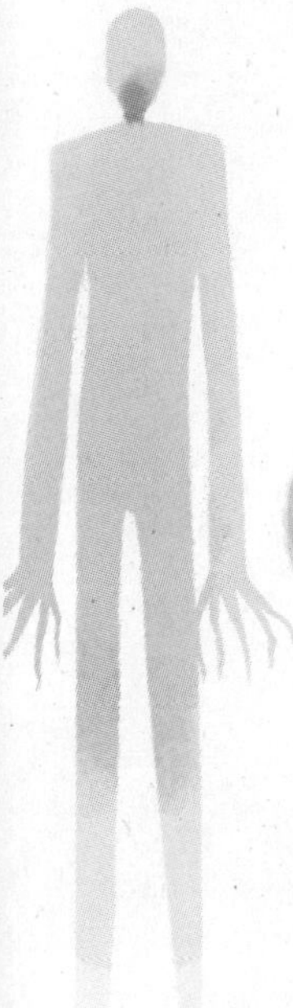

SCHOLASTIC'S ULTIMATE

GHOST STORIES

Illustrated by

MODEERA FATIMA

SCHOLASTIC
New York Toronto London Auckland
Sydney New Delhi Hong Kong

SCHOLASTIC'S ULTIMATE GHOST STORIES

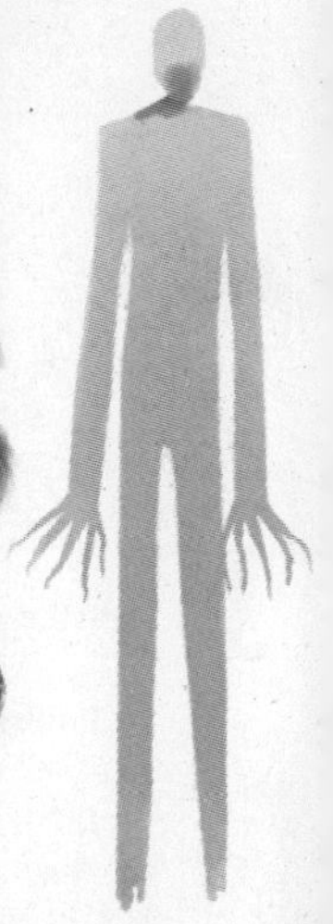

Revised collection edited by Ashley Kumar and Prerna Mathur

Published by Scholastic India Pvt. Ltd.
A subsidiary of Scholastic Inc., New York, 10012 (USA).
Publishers since 1920, with international operations in Canada, Australia, New Zealand, the United Kingdom, India, and Hong Kong.

For information regarding permission, write to:
Scholastic India Pvt. Ltd.
A-27, Ground Floor, Sigma Centre
Infocity-1, Sector 34, Gurgaon-122001 (India)

First edition: September 2025

ISBN-13: 978-93-5954-947-7

Printed in India at: VK Global Digital Private Limited

CONTENTS

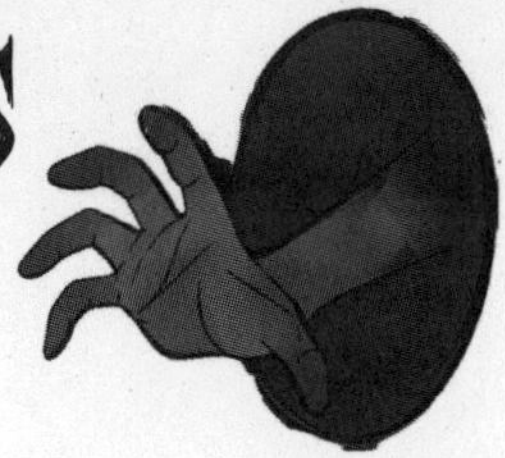

THE SHADOW PEOPLE

Meenakshi Reddy Madhavan

When Yamini stepped out at Vilasgunj station, she was surprised to see that there was no one there. Even for a small town—well, perhaps, *because* it was a small town—Vilasgunj had a surprisingly busy station. There was a magazine man and an oranges woman and usually Anant Ram, the old, wizened station master, who knew everybody. But today it seemed abandoned and all Yamini could see were the twisting shadows from the trees. She was even more surprised that for the first time in her life, nobody had come to receive her. It was her first day back from boarding school, it was the *holidays*, and she had a trunk and couldn't be expected to carry it all the way home. Well, at least she thought she had a trunk.

Yamini watched in astonishment as the train pulled out of the station leaving absolutely nothing behind. 'Hey!' she yelled, running after it, 'Hey! My trunk!' Nope. There was no indication of the train stopping or even anyone listening to her. This was a very bad day, and Yamini set her teeth, preparing to go home and complain to her mother. Then she would be fed mangoes, and she would play with the dogs and maybe in the evening, go swimming with her cousins. Nothing was so bad that it ruined the summer holidays. It was probably a mix up, she said to herself comfortingly. They probably expect me tomorrow, and how surprised they'll be to see me walk in and everyone will feel really bad for me. She smiled to herself at the thought of the adults' aghast faces. She could milk this for a while.

The fact that ghosts come out at night is a myth, just like many other things in this world. They still retain some of their human traits and like to sleep like the rest of us. There are scary things that appear in the middle of the night—monsters and werewolves and things wanting revenge—but, god preserve us, not ghosts.

Maybe she could get a lift along the way, thought Yamini. Having lived her entire life in Vilasgunj at 'Chaudhury ka bungalow' people knew her and her family. She was confident that anyone seeing her trudging along in the heat would stop and offer to drop her home. The bungalow was about two kilometres away and her shoes hurt as the sun beat down on her hair. But the rest of the town was as empty as the station. Was it a festival day? Sometimes people retired to their houses on special occasions, spending time with their families till the evening when they made house calls and distributed sweets. Her family was quite involved with all town happenings, and if it *was* a festival day, then that would explain why they had forgotten to pick her up. Yamini tried not to get too frustrated with the heat and her shoes and her confusion. It would be better soon. She just wanted her mother.

Walking home, Yamini felt somehow like she was in a dream. Not a good dream, or even necessarily, a nightmare, just one of those dreams where you float around and everything seems sort of surreal. She put it down to the baking heat, and felt her forehead to see if she was getting a fever. That gesture once again reminded her of her mother, oh, how surprised they'd all be when she got home, maybe she'd be put to bed, with the AC roaring and someone to check in on her, feed her mangoes from a plate. She didn't feel warm though, despite the sun, she felt cool, as though she had been indoors all day.

Most ghosts are pretty angry that there is no heaven. There is no hell either, but no one really thinks they're going to hell. Instead they are locked to earth, as much as they were when they were alive and there's nowhere else for them to go.

Yamini finally reached the large bungalow where her family lived. She had described it to a school friend earlier that term as, 'the biggest house in the town'. This was not technically true. Yamini's house was not the biggest, but it had the largest spread. Most houses were built vertically, four or five storeys, in a concession to modernity, but hers sprawled around a courtyard with a well, and each of the four walls surrounding the courtyard had rooms that served different purposes. Yamini's family lived in the side that faced west and she could watch the sunset every evening from her room. When she had been younger, she asked her mother why sunsets had to happen. 'I want the day to go on and on,' she had said, her face mutinous. Her mother had laughed, a little sadly, and said, 'The sun has to go spend time with other people now, baby.' Later, her father had pulled out his old globe and demonstrated to her how the earth moved and how the sun shifted locations, but she had liked her mother's explanation better. Maybe they had gone to spend time with other people, too. Maybe they had forgotten all about her.

The old gate creaked as she pushed through it and with one last burst of energy she ran inside the house. 'Ma? Papa? I'm home!' she yelled as she ran from room to room. 'Chutki?' she called for her little sister, 'It's me, Yamini!' The house was empty, abandoned, but it didn't feel abandoned. It felt as though they had just stepped out for a moment and would be back soon. The cows mooed from the cow shed at her voice and she ran there to look for her father, her uncle, anyone. But there was no one there. The house waited quietly. In a burst of tears, Yamini ran into her room and wept.

Trouble maker ghosts are the origins of all ghost stories. Your grandmother wouldn't come back to haunt you. Sure, she watches you every now and then, but, then, like a soap opera you've given up on, you lose track of characters and then you just stop caring.

Yamini had fallen asleep crying and when she woke up, the sun had already set and she heard some faint murmurs from the rest of the house. Thinking it was her family back again, she got up a little groggily, and made her way outside. The house was dark, no lights on, but she could feel the closeness of people. She tried to switch on a light, but it didn't work. Yamini was a brave girl, used to frequent power cuts and not afraid of very much, having grown up with very sensible parents who reasoned her out of any imaginary frights, and many boy cousins who had tried pranks on her and failed. No electricity? Just light a candle, which she did, and began to move to the northward set of rooms. That was where the kitchen was and the dining room, and where the family gathered at the end of the day. The murmurs grew as she approached the dining room, but when she threw open the door, once more it was empty.

Or was it?

In front of Yamini's eyes, she watched her shadow leap in the candlelight and then she saw four or five other shadows joining it. There were people in this room. The

wind murmured low in the trees outside, but perhaps it wasn't the wind. It was whispering noises, noises that made no sense when you confronted them, but if you closed your eyes, noises that were conversations. She gripped tightly onto her candle holder, watching as the shadows moved independently. One of the shadows noticed her, and before she could make a sound, grabbed on to her shadow and dragged it into the courtyard. And this time, *Yamini* was the shadow. She was forced to go along with her dark image, dragged as if they were sewn together at the feet, her hands shook and she dropped the candle, and she looked down and felt her body grow weirdly. It was as if she was looking into one of those 'fun' mirrors, she morphed into a creature with long flapping arms, her shoulder and torso grew very tall and her legs fused together so she couldn't walk.

But she didn't need to walk anymore, she was being pulled by her shadow into the courtyard and there around the well, she finally saw people. Dev, a second cousin who had drowned in this very well, Ayah who died when Yamini was about ten and who had worked for the family since Yamini's mother was a little girl, Dada, her grandfather who she had never met, but whose picture hung in the kitchen. For the first time in her life, Yamini felt a little flicker of fear.

These were ... *go on, say it* ... but it was impossible ... *not impossible if you can see them* ... these were ... *dead people.*

The dead people around the well turned to her and smiled, and Ayah, who was the one who had grabbed Yamini's shadow, let it go. Yamini watched as it bounced towards her and then gasped as it bounced into her. Her legs separated, then fused, then separated again. Her stomach clenched and she thought she was going to vomit, and then her body shrank massively and she was thrown to the ground. When she stood up a little dazed, she looked down and noticed she could see the grass and the stones and the moonlight shine through her body. She was flat, uni-dimensional. She was, in short, her shadow.

'Why are you here?' she squeaked, 'Where is my family? What has happened to me?'

'Dear Yamini,' said Dada, his own shadow self flickering by the well. 'Your family is well. They're inside.'

'No, they're not!' she screamed. 'They're not, they're not, they're not! What have you done with them?'

'Yamini, beta,' Ayah stepped towards her. 'You're a shadow person now.'

'But I don't *want* to be a shadow person! Let me go!'

'Go then,' said Dev, smiling. 'Go run inside and find your mummy-daddy and they'll tell you this is all a dream. Go on!'

'Dev!' said Dada, sternly.

'What? If she wants to go, send her. I have other things to do than sit around and listen to her scream.'

'Dev, it's not easy for anyone,' said Ayah.

'Well,' said Dev, still looking annoyed, 'I've been a Shadow Person longer than you have, and frankly, I'm a little bored of having to go over the explanations over and over again.'

Yamini didn't stop to hear anymore. She raced through her house, going, 'Ma! Mumma! Please come out!' until she had been everywhere and they were nowhere and once more she was facing the three ghosts.

'*Not* ghosts,' said Dada. '*Shadow* people.'

Yamini went over to a bench and sat down. If ghost was the same as a shadow person, if they had called her a shadow person, it meant that ... 'Am I a ghost?' she asked.

'Shadow person!' said Dev, looking crosser.

'Ayah?' said Yamini, her lower lip beginning to quiver.

'Darling girl,' said Ayah, her wonderful comforting face making Yamini feel much better, 'We are all shadow people. Even your parents.'

Wild hope leaped up in Yamini. 'Can I see *them*?' she asked. Dev laughed mockingly and Dada made his form stretch till it reached the top floor. 'Dev! One more peep out of you, and I will have you banished from the grounds for fifty years.'

'Not like I want to stay anyway,' muttered Dev, but he shut up.

'There are two kinds of shadow people,' said Dada.

'The ones who breathe and the ones who don't. We can only see each other. The breathers can only see each other also. Once in a great while, a non breather and breather will be able to meet, but these instances are rare.'

'But I breathe,' said Yamini.

Ayah's eyes were kind as they rested on her face. 'Try,' she said.

Yamini realised she had been holding her breath this entire time, and oddly, she didn't feel the funny bursting feeling she normally did. She exhaled and inhaled and then began to cough. She only regained herself once she took in a mouthful of air and held her breath. It felt, weirdly, natural.

'What does this mean?' she asked, and then she knew. 'Am I dead?'

'*Finally!*' said Dev, 'I thought you were going to take forever, and we aren't allowed to tell you, you have to figure it out for yourself. Yes, you're dead, you died on your way to catch a train back home. Run over by a bus.' He made a flattening motion with his hand. 'Shmush. Dead. Like roadkill.'

Dada's eyes flashed and Dev shrunk, suddenly half his size.

'She had to know!' he squeaked.

Yamini thought back. Funnily, she couldn't remember getting on the train, or even the journey. She had assumed she had slept the whole way, but she would have surely had some memory of it.

'There is no heaven,' Ayah began and the other two joined in, speaking low, like they were chanting:

There is no heaven, there is no hell. The world is what it is.

Breathers hear us, we hear breathers, but we can never meet.

Shadows live, under breather's feet, until the breather is no more.

Shadows wait, dancing in the light, to take you where they were.

Then shadow and breather combine, and we are one.

We are Shadow People.

The hair on Yamini's arms stood straight up. The courtyard was flooded with light and shadows. The whispers came back. *We are Shadow People*, said the trees and the wind. *We are Shadow People*, murmured the other figures, suddenly everywhere. I am dead, thought Yamini, and her body began to glow in the moonlight, I am dead and I am a shadow person.

It's funny how nothing seemed to matter anymore. Not the ghosts of wails she could hear from inside the house or the year—or was it a hundred—that passed her by.

THEN THERE WAS ONE

Jane De Suza

A fist punching my shoulder woke me up. 'Hey Sissy, let's see how brave you are. We're going into the hill tunnel. Get out of bed.' My watch showed one in the morning and the tent was pitch black inside except for the face of my tormentor, Raghu, ghostly in the green light of my watch, shaking me awake.

Okay, some background first, I guess. I am eleven, thin and, you know, the non-sporty kind. The thickest thing about me is my glasses. Obviously then, my folks, in some misguided attempt to toughen me up, sent me to this week-long adventure camp. Almost at once, I became the favourite punching bag of a rough gang of 14-year-old hulks: Akhil with biceps like logs, Sam who was built like a truck, and Raghu, who was the worst kind of nasty, who'd pin a butterfly's wings down.

The camp put us through some cliff-climbing, rapelling and that sort of stuff. We had set up tents in a forest clearing; and on one trek, when we got kind of lost on a hill, we had stumbled upon an old wooden door, hidden by long grass, in the hillside rock. The locals never went near it—it led to some unholy stuff, they said. They left little pots of sweets or garlands outside the door to appease whichever angry demonic force lived within.

On the last night of camp, when Raghu woke me up, I was so exhausted and so happy to be going home, I didn't fight it anymore. 'Okay,' I said, 'I'm not scared. Let's go'. I'd prove to them that I was no baby.

So, on that moonless night, the four of us picked our way across the brambles scratching our legs, up to the hill and to the hidden door. The others kept prodding me along. 'Hey Missy, got your night facecream on? You look pale.'

We found the small door and tried to push it open. No. Sam put his huge shoulder against it. No. We all began to kick it then, till, with a blood-curdling whine, it creaked open. We looked at each other. No one had really expected it to open. It was tar-black inside.

'Go in first, Sissy!' Raghu hissed. I looked around, worried, but the three mocking faces, with eyes glinting, made my mind up for me. So I got onto my knees and crawled in. The tunnel was only about the height of a small boy, and so we had to crouch. I heard the others following me. We had no torches, except for the light out of our watches.

Wham! We screamed because it was just so sudden, yes, all four of us. Swivelling around, we saw that the hillside door had shut. Akhil, who was last, moved over to it and tried to open it. We all pushed. It wouldn't budge at all. We pulled and kicked, then with a knot in our stomachs, decided to just move on. Maybe the tunnel would lead out of another door?

That's when we first heard it. A faraway lonely horn, the sort that an old trumpet or wind pipe would make. 1- 2 - 3 - 4. Four blasts of a rusty old horn coming from somewhere deep within the hillside. But it couldn't be 4 o'clock. It had been barely half an hour since we'd left. What was that horn counting?

The tunnel sloped upwards sharply, and so we were out of breath in a few minutes. In the dark, lit up by eerie green watch lights, gasping along, I felt something brush against my face. 'No!' I gasped. Was it a bat? A moth? Or that supposed hill demon? The others tried to laugh, piteously, frightened themselves.

Another gasp. This time it wasn't me. It came from the back of our troop. Akhil stuttered, 'No. No. Oh please no!'

'What is it, dude?' We turned around trying to focus our watch lights on him. Had he fallen and injured himself?

Weird! Where was he? There was just no Akhil. There was only a frightened Raghu behind me, and a shivering Sam. No Akhil at the rear.

'Akhil!' we called out. No answer. We tried to train our watch lights on the walls—a hidden side-tunnel maybe. Nothing.

Then the horn began to blow slowly and sadly again. 1 - 2 - 3.

'It's counting us,' I whispered. 'That horn blew four times for four of us. Now, it's blowing only thrice.'

Our hearts were beating so loudly, we could probably hear each other's. Raghu pushed me and sent

me sprawling forward. 'Go! Go you little idiot! Move it! Move on! Run!'

My knee had cut from the fall, and I could feel warm blood dripping down my leg. Oh god, let there be no blood-sucking beast in here which would nose me out. My eyes fogged up behind my glasses and I pushed my way upwards. My legs were aching and my ribcage throbbing but I pushed on.

Raghu hissed. 'Let's put the scaredy-poo at the back, Sam. Let him get picked off next by whatever demon this is.'

I scrambled up the tunnel rockface desperately. Raghu's hand shot out and tried to grab my ankle, but I kicked out frantically.

'Ow!' Raghu called out. 'You little creep. I'll get you. I'll wring your neck, I'll ...'

A loud cackle cut into his threats. The tunnel began to echo with eerie cackling—a rusty old laugh that went on and on. The hollow tunnel reverberated with it, multiplying it many times over till it surrounded us.

I sobbed, and tried to pull myself on. I'd read a lot of books. I could name about a dozen different evil spirits, but they were not real. Not real, I tried to remind myself.

They were just imaginary—imagined up by writers the world over. There was no demonic force. I would win this race just on my intellect—I had more brains than those bullies behind me combined. There. Was. No. Evil. Force. I told myself. But then—where did Akhil disappear? What was that horn? What was that cackling?

Another brush of something across my cheek, followed by a cackling laugh again. All three of us screamed, and the screams joined the echoing laughter.

When the noise finally stopped, and all that was audible was our sobbing, we pushed onwards and upwards with a sudden frantic energy we didn't even know we had. I forgot the pain of cut knees, bruised knuckles, and just climbed up, over rocky, wet, slimy rockface in that dark tunnel.

We pushed on, sobbing, praying, whispering that we'd never do anything like this again. No playing hookie. No ...

'My watch light's gone,' whispered Sam. 'Raghu, will you stop pulling at my neck!'

Raghu replied. 'I'm not. I'm ahead of you.'

Sam said in a gush of words, 'Then who is dragging me by my neck? Who's behind me? Akhil—is that you? Oh my god, what is that? What ...'

His voice just stopped abruptly. Raghu and I swung backwards to see nothing. Sam, blubbering and sobbing, had quietened down. We couldn't hear him anymore, and couldn't see him either.

I gulped. This could not be happening.

But it was! The horn began to blow mournfully. 1 - 2. Just two.

'Raghu, pinch me. It's a dream. I'm going home tomorrow,' I cried. I was just a little boy and I wanted to go home to my folks, to my little sister, to my books. I wanted to wake up from this nightmare.

Raghu lunged at me and pinched my ear hard. He twisted it around too, till I yelled.

'Is that enough for you, Sissy?' he whispered angrily. 'You think this is some game, you idiot? Something out of your fairy tale books?'

I found some inner core of steel I didn't even know I had and pulled myself upwards again. Climbing up, my hands reaching out to the rock and pulling myself upwards, gasping, awash in sweat.

Raghu gasped behind me. 'Wait, you idiot. Don't you dare try to get away from me. I'm not going to die in this place. It's you next!'

He reached out and grabbed at my leg and I tried to shake him off, kick him off, but he'd caught on this time. I felt his fingers wrap around my ankle. 'No!' I cried. 'Don't, please!'

Raghu pulled himself up so that we were both at the same level in that upward sloping tunnel. He grabbed my upper arm, and hissed, 'You go to the back.'

'No. Raghu, listen. We're the only two left. This demon is taking whoever is at the back. And then one of us will be alone.' I cried, frantically trying to find some way to get out of this on my brainpower, to save us, to save myself. 'Look, if we both stick together, there won't be any one at the back or front. This evil thing can't pick us out if we're both together. No one at the back, okay?'

I could see from the fading light of Raghu's watch, since mine had faded away too, that he was trying to make up his mind.

The eerie laughter began again and that seemed to do it. Raghu gripped me, digging into the flesh of my arm. 'Okay, go! Let's try it your way. Together. Go!'

Together, we pushed up, forcing our way through strings of what was cold, misty, clammy water? Spider webs? Cutting our elbows and knees on the rock—

pushing upwards, dreading the next pealing of the horn.

Why did we have to come in here? I wished I had just stayed in bed, and had not tried to prove anything. I thought of my little sister waiting for me to come home from camp and forced back another sob. I had to get out of this alive. I had to.

Somewhere deep down, I felt it was useless. The demonic forces of the hill were claiming their victims. We were their prey. We had invaded their privacy, their homes kept secret for probably centuries—and here we were, silly schoolboys stumbling upon ancient secrets. They would not let us go.

Raghu let out a yell. 'What the ...! My foot!' He shouted in pain. 'My foot is caught!' We looked down, and his foot was lodged in some sort of hole in the ground. Oh my god, is this how the others had disappeared? Through some holes in the tunnel—into the hillside—to lie buried forever?

'Pull me out!' Raghu cried, and I stared at him. This was the guy who had made my week at camp a living hell. He had tormented me, bullied me, made me cry, made me look like a fool in front of everyone—so many times. I could leave him there and let the demon of the hill claim its next victim. I turned forward and upwards to leave. Then I stopped.

I couldn't.

All that was decent and good within me stopped me from moving ahead. I knew it was my only hope to go it alone, but I couldn't. I couldn't just leave him to die there.

Choking back a sob, because I knew it was back to the battle of the two of us again—I reached out my thin arms and grabbed him around the chest. He heaved and I heaved and with another yell, his foot pulled out.

Raghu was breathing heavily and crying openly. This big bully. If only the other boys at camp could see him now. 'I almost went, man, I almost died out there. You saved me, man.'

'It's okay, Raghu, let's just go on,' I said. 'Together, remember?'

Then over our sobs, came the long, sad, blood-curdling blowing of the horn. Clearly. Once. Just one long siren. We waited for the next. For 2. Silence. There was just one. One of us would go.

We looked at each other terrified. A cold clammy hand of fear slid down my spine. This was it. One of us was going to be sacrificed now. Disappear forever. To appease the demons of the hill.

'It's not going to be me,' hissed Raghu, his eyes narrow and glinting in the fading green light of his watch, and he grabbed my shoulder and pushed me back—back into that hole into which he'd almost fallen.

'No, no, Raghu, no!' I screamed, but I was no match for his huge bulk. I felt myself falling and the last thing I saw above me was Raghu's face, evil glimmering out of his eyes. And it struck me—it wasn't just pure evil inside the hillside, there was evil hiding in each one of us; it's just that in many of us, the good won over the evil.

Everything was black. I fell, tumbling, rolling, my back and legs scraping against rock, screaming, praying, lower and lower, until I saw I was tumbling towards an orange light. A fire? Oh my god, this was the fire within the belly of the mountain. I was falling to my death—to the demon's cave? To their furnace?

You read in these circumstances how people black out, right? That would have been merciful. But I was conscious of every long drawn moment.

Finally, I fell out into that light, eyes shut out of sheer fear of what I would find myself in. I wasn't ready to confront the demons of the hillside, I was absolutely terrified. There was a lot of shouting and I steeled myself for whatever was coming next. Slowly I opened my eyes.

I was out on the hillside again, I had fallen right through the tunnel out of a hole in the hill. I found the camp coaches and other students and locals clustered around me with torches—that explained the light at the end of the tunnel. There was a search party out looking for us. I almost fainted in the arms of the coach.

In all the hushed silence, I heard the old voice of the local chief. 'This is the one that survived.'

I looked back at the hill and in my head, I heard the screaming, the cackling, the eerie laughter, the horn. Where had the others disappeared? Had they too escaped out of holes in the hillside, or had the hill demons claimed them?

A week later, when all the media excitement had died down, I held my little sister close to me on our verandah swing, while I went through the file of newspaper clippings about my 'miraculous' escape. The other three boys had never been found. And the door in the hillside had vanished. No one ever found it again.

The Book

Samhita Arni

Many, many years ago, I chanced upon a strange, little bookshop in Old Town. It was a ramshackle operation, stacks of books lined the pavement, moulting pages in the noonday sun, arranged haphazardly—*The Communist Manifesto* keeping company with *The Wind in the Willows*, and Polidori's *Vampyre* lying precariously close to Austen's *Mansfield Park*, pages touching. I chuckled to myself, imagining what havoc was to unfold if Polidori's bloodsucking protagonist were to leap out of the covers and jump across pages, to sink his teeth into Lady Bertram's beloved Pug. Catastrophe would result, with a vampiric pug chasing down the corridors of Mansfield Park—turning all our beloved (and not so beloved) characters—Fanny, Edward, Henry Crawford, Ms Norris—into creatures of the night.

As I examined the contents of another pile, I stumbled across a strange book. It was a tiny thing, with an ancient, black threadbare cover, leaves spilling out. I opened the book, and glanced across the first page. There was nothing—just a blank page. Puzzled, I flipped past pages until I came, in the middle of the book, to a white page, marred by a single black dot.

The dot grew, before my very eyes, it spread across the page and resolved itself into a picture, in the manner of a black and white etching.

It was a portrait of a young woman, who looked strangely familiar. As I looked at the picture, her features withered, her eyes grew rheumy, and lines etched themselves in the corner of her mouth. She was now, perhaps, in her late fifties, and even as I watched, the edges of the page began to burn and char, fire creeping slowly towards the center of the image. The woman

looked at either side, at the burning edges that framed her, imprisoned her, and fear began to twist her features, furrow her brow. Her features melted into a pool of black ink, as her face began to burn, and her mouth opened in a soundless scream.

I shut the book.

The smell of burning still hung in the air, and my heart rocked in my chest. I shut my eyes, hoping to erase the image of her burning face, but it was still there, etched in darkness against my eyelids. I opened my eyes, shocked now, for I had realised why her features had been so familiar, why her face had tugged at my memory.

'Are you alright?' A voice sounded by my ear. I turned, it was a fellow customer, a sandy haired tourist, perusing the stacks of books on the pavement. I nodded and moved away, into the shop.

It was dark inside; it smelt of mothballs, dusty old pages and paan. I went to the cashier's desk, but there was only a little boy sleeping there, his head resting on a thick volume of Shakespeare.

'Is someone older here? Who owns this shop?' I asked, a little surprised. The boy shook his head, rubbing the sleep from his eyes.

'No, my grandfather is away, but you can pay here.' I sighed, I didn't imagine that this little boy would be much help in learning anything about the black book in my hands. 'When will your grandfather be back?' I asked.

The little boy shrugged, and then turning to a dark doorway behind him, shouted, 'Ammi!'

A woman answered, faintly, something I couldn't catch. As I waited, she emerged from the doorway, a pretty girl, I could tell, even in the darkness of the shop. She had almond shaped grey eyes, heavily lined with kohl, and a fair, smooth skin.

As she came in, she pulled her pink scarf over her hair, and her bangles jingled, a soft, sweet sound. She seemed very young, too young to have birthed the boy beside her. I was caught by her beauty, the beauty of an houri or a princess, a strange thing to find in the darkness of a bookshop.

The boy showed her the book. She frowned at the book, but didn't touch it, or glance at the pages. Smiling sweetly at me, she replied in beautiful, classical Urdu. 'I'm sorry, I can't help you. But my father will be back, next week, he's gone to his village.'

I bought the book, in any case, and left the shop. I opened it, many times in the following days, but it only ever showed me one picture, the picture I had already seen.

Months passed, and the book was lying, forgotten, in a drawer, when my nephew, a sweet six-year-old, came to stay with me. His parents, jet-setting executives, had little time to spend with their boy, and so he often came to me. He was a quiet, frail thing and we would work in comfortable silence together, he—industriously colouring little pictures of houses and families—and me, trying hard to transmute simple words and sentences into something much greater, into stories, plots and characters.

One day, though, the silence was broken by a little cry. I turned around, and found the black book in his hands. He had torn out a leaf, and before our eyes, black smoke was unfurling across the page, black flowers blossoming, petals wilting, dissolving. I snatched the page from his little hands, and watched rivers and lakes of ink shape into a picture.

What I saw broke my heart.

'I just wanted a piece of paper for a picture,' he lisped at me, thinking his quest for paper had occasioned my anger. I couldn't speak then, tears were choking my throat. I clutched him and buried my face in his nest of curly hair.

'Why are you crying?' he asked. I couldn't tell him.

That night I couldn't sleep, but watched the rise and fall of his chest, as he dreamt. What did he dream? What did six-year-old boys dream of?

It was too much to bear.

My sister came, a couple of days later, to pick up her little son. 'You should spend more time with him,' I told her, gathering his toys together.

My sister wrenched his things out of my hands. 'It's all very well for you to say,' she sneered at me, her voice rising, 'You don't have a job.' As I started in surprise, she went on, 'Well ... not a regular job, not like the rest of us. And you don't have a kid either. Children are expensive—schools, tuitions, nannies, field trips, summer camp—we have to save for college as well.' She stormed off, pushing things quickly into his suitcase.

She didn't speak to me for a week.

Perhaps it wouldn't happen, I told myself. Perhaps the book was wrong.

Some time later, I had a couple of friends over for dinner. It was a pleasant evening, and as darkness descended, we uncorked a bottle of wine. It was a night full of stars, and as we sat outside, a friend began to tell a story about a haunted house he had lived in. It was a lovely tale, and after that, emboldened by the magic of the evening and the wine, I started to talk of the black book.

One of my closest friends, an actor, dismissed my story with a sweep of his beautiful, elegant hand, and an expression of derision spreading across his face. 'No! No!' he cried, 'that's not a story at all. You're a writer—you've got to come up with something better! With characters, with plot, mystery and ambition! This is nothing ... too much like Dorian Gray ...' I was hurt by his flamboyant disapproval, I was a little in love with him then, many of us were.

Perhaps it was that which made me a little angry.

Incensed, I replied that it wasn't a story, that it was something true. My audience guffawed, and to prove them wrong, I rushed into my bedroom and pulled out the book.

My actor friend pried the book loose from my hands. I watched his perfect, handsome profile, outlined against the moon, as he flipped through the pages, and watched his smile droop, the light fade from his eyes.

'What is it?' I asked. A strange silence fell over the gathering, as he shut the book, and handed it back to me.

'Nothing, nothing,' he tried to smile, but failed.

I felt a brief flutter of disappointment mingled with guilt—had it been anger, or the wine, that had egged me on? I watched him as he moved away and pulled out a cigarette. As the match flared, the fire lit his face briefly—and I saw something in his expression, that I hadn't seen before—weariness, sadness, disgust? I couldn't tell.

Months later, he lay, sick and wasted, on a hospital bed, diagnosed with AIDS. 'Too much loving,' he told me, a smile twisting his withered lips. I wanted to ask him then, what he had seen in the book, but he turned towards the wall and coughed, blood spewing from his lungs, sores puckering his face. I never got the chance to ask him again.

Ten years passed by.

My sister had moved to the States, years ago, when my nephew had been a scant seven years old. I wanted to tell her then what I had seen, but as the words hovered on my tongue, she spoke first.

'I know what you're going to say,' she told me, 'keep it for yourself. You're not a mother, you don't know what it's like.' She turned, and marched towards her plane.

In America, her family grew, and they prospered—they acquired a house in the country, a number of cars, American citizenship. She made it sound like a perfect life.

But one day, she called me, just as darkness fled from the morning sky. 'He's gone,' she wept, static punctuating her sobs. 'He died, a few hours ago.' Returning from work the previous evening, they had found him, wrists slit, floating in rose-tinted bathwater. It had been too late. The story came out, they—she and her husband—hadn't approved of his clothes, of his friends, of his dreams. 'We didn't understand him,' she cried. I couldn't think of anything to say—I knew they didn't, they hadn't understood him as a six-year-old.

I sat in silence, as day gathered into dusk, and I wondered what I could have said to change things.

And as the call to evening prayer sounded, I pulled on my shoes, and headed for Old Town. I had come here, many times, searching for the same bookshop—but Old Town was a warren of tiny, dark streets, and it was impossible for me to find anything here.

But today I was determined. Perhaps I had to convince myself that I was not guilty. In any case, I chased children as they traipsed across the roofs and alleys of Old Town, watched pigeons swirl high against an orange sky, and listened to the awesome beauty of a imam's prayer, hurtling through a loudspeaker perched on a minaret.

And then I found it, stumbling, almost by mistake, onto the same piles of books lying jumbled on the pavement, just as they had been all those years ago. There was the same darkness inside the shop, the same grimy, yellowing volume of Shakespeare peeking out from under the counter.

Only now, the counter was manned by a young man, smoking a foul smelling cheroot, film music blaring from a mobile phone clipped to his jeans' pocket. Stubble clung to his face, and behind him, on the wall, I could discern a few pictures, torn from magazines—Salman, Dino, Shah Rukh, the familiar catalogue of film stars.

'Please,' I had asked timidly, 'is the shop owner here?'

He had glared at me, chewing on his cheroot. I pulled out the black book, and showed it to him. 'I bought this ten, eleven years ago, from this shop. I wanted to know ... where it was from.' I gave him a desperate, fervent look, and thought of my nephew, lying palms spread out, in a tub of tepid water.

Something in my expression must have persuaded him, for he turned towards the doorway behind him, and again, like before, shouted 'Ammi!'

And she appeared now, much older.

Her prettiness had faded, her once smooth skin was now mottled and wrinkled. White streaked her hair, but her eyes were just the same—beautiful, grey, almond-shaped eyes—the eyes of a princess, of an houri.

And again, there was the smile—the heart-breaking, beautiful smile.

I placed the book before her. 'I bought this book from this shop many years ago. I was wondering whether anyone could tell me something about it.'

She shook her head. 'If only you had come a few weeks ago,' she said, 'my father died last week. This was his shop, he knew everything about the books here.'

I smiled, regretfully, turning to go, but a thought occurred. 'If you don't mind me asking—how did he die?' I asked.

'Cancer,' she had said. 'Of the lungs. He always said that smoking was going to kill him.' She smiled again, 'It's strange how he knew that.'

That was some time ago. Now, I watch my face age, watch lines incise themselves onto my skin, watch my cheeks droop, my lips wither. I am growing old, everyone grows old, but I wait for the day when my face will match the face I saw, I still see, in the black book. I keep the book beside me, waiting.

I wait for the fire to come and melt my face, and char the pages of the book.

MIRROR-SELF

Payal Dhar

The only thing Jiya knew about her grandfather was that when he died, her grandmother threw away all the mirrors in her house. She went to see her grandmother at least once a year—mostly during the summer holidays—and must have explored her house top to bottom a thousand times without ever coming across a mirror.

'Appa, why doesn't Paati have mirrors?' she asked her father often.

But Appa only rolled his eyes and said, 'Don't ask.'

So mostly Jiya didn't ask. She loved her Paati very much and basked in the knowledge that she was her favourite granddaughter. She even knew why—it was because she read so much. Paati loved to read too. She had over a thousand books in the 'library' room, and rumour had it that when she was younger, Paati used to write as well.

'What did you write about?' Jiya asked her one time.

'About the truth,' her grandmother replied, after a few moments' thought.

'Oh,' said Jiya, thinking. She had been nine then, about two years ago. 'You mean, you were a journalist?'

Jiya knew all about journalists. Both Amma and Appa worked in the media.

But Paati only laughed and hugged her. 'No, my dear.'

'But why don't you write any more?' persisted Jiya. 'I'd like to read your stories. Were they stories? It doesn't matter, because I like to read all kinds of things. Can I read your stories?'

Then Paati got all serious. 'No, child, you can't. They are too dangerous.'

That sent a thrill up Jiya's spine. How could reading be dangerous? But Paati wouldn't say any more, except mutter something about 'as long as your Thatha was alive.'

While Jiya, her brother, Babu, and their cousins often stayed at Paati's home, she only consented to having them as long as at least one parent stayed. 'I can't manage a group of boisterous children,' she would say irritably.

One of the more malicious aunts whispered something about how the old lady had been slowly losing it after Thatha died, but no one dared openly defy Paati. The only grandchild Paati consented to having with her without any other supervision was Jiya herself. Not even Babu was included. That made Jiya the object of envy among the others, but she didn't care. She loved the house and more than anything else, she loved having Paati all to herself.

But the year that she turned eleven was the last time she stayed there alone.

It was a really old house—older than Paati, and she was so old that she didn't remember her age. Looking up at the ceiling made Jiya dizzy, and she was sometimes scared of the beams running across them. They creaked in complaint with the weight of the fans, and a few times Jiya and Babu had seen squirrels dart in from the garden, sprint across the beams and back, like it was some sort of a dare among themselves.The windows in the house were wide and long, with wooden shutters. Jiya once found it great fun to open and shut the slats of the shutters, but after getting her finger caught she now steered clear of them. The only odd thing about the house was the absence of mirrors. It was exceedingly inconvenient. How was one supposed to brush one's hair, for instance? There was only so much you could do with shiny surfaces and backs of steel plates.

Every afternoon after lunch Paati would shut the windows and pull down the shutters in her bedroom. The room would become dark and then magically cool. Almost as if the scorching summer outside had been banned from entering. Then Paati would perch on her large bed and kick off her slippers. She would take off her glasses, put them on the bedside table, then place her keys next to them. Then she would slowly lie back. Her eyes closed, she would say: 'Jiya, come, lie down for a bit.'

It had always been like that, every day, without fail. And every day, equally without fail, Jiya would wait till her grandmother started snoring softly and then sneak away. Those two hours that Paati slept was when Jiya lived many adventures—she saved lives, fought aliens, walked on the moon, trawled the oceans for treasure.

The underneath of the gigantic dining table (Paati and Thatha had had seven children!) functioned variously as a secret tunnel, an underground den, the deep seas, a swimming pool, a clearing in a forest, a hut in a rainstorm. A sheet draped over two chairs was her alpine tent where she huddled on cold treacherous nights when the wind screamed outside and wild animals roamed. The heavy bulky furniture formed a dangerous route through enemy territory ...

The opportunities were endless. She could be an adventurer, a spy, a detective. She conquered mountains, battled wild beasts and hoodwinked dastardly criminals. A new idea was only a book away, and there were plenty of those about.

But this time it was different. This time Jiya was on a mission: she was going to find out about the mirrors, and she figured that it all had something to do with her grandmother's abandoned writings. A thorough and methodical search of the house—under the pretext of playing adventure games—had led her to the conclusion that whatever secrets lay hidden were inside the room next to her Paati's which was kept locked all the time.

Just before she crept out of the bedroom that fateful afternoon, Jiya made a quick detour to the bedside table and carefully lifted the bunch of keys from the yellowing crocheted cover. She placed a hand under it to keep it from jangling, and watched with bated breath to see if Paati would wake. She didn't, and Jiya escaped.

It was easy to match the number of the golden coloured key that fit the large Godrej padlock. The key turned smooth as butter and before she knew it, Jiya was in what she now thought of as Paati's secret room. And it was such a disappointment.

It was so small that Jiya could almost touch the walls on both sides if she stretched her arms out. About half a dozen steps and she would reach the other end of the narrow room. It was more like a little blind corridor than a room. There were no windows, but strangely there wasn't that musty smell that Jiya remembered when they returned home after a long holiday and the house had been shut up. The room was completely bare except for a rusted metal trunk pushed up against the far wall and a folding ladder—the kind Amma and Appa used to change bulbs or clean the fans. The floor was clean and cool under her bare feet.

Jiya's only hope now was the trunk, but when she went to it, she saw that it had a combination lock. She felt disappointed and annoyed. All that creeping around, and all for nothing. She gave the ladder a little shake in frustration, and as she took another glance around, she looked up at the off-white whitewashed walls reaching up to the ceiling. And something inside her gave a little lurch of excitement.

This ceiling wasn't as high as the others in the house, but there was a loft on the wall to her left. And from where she stood, she could see stacks and stacks of notebooks.

In a frenzy of excitement, Jiya grabbed the ladder and after struggling with it for a while, managed to open it up. She placed it by the wall and climbed up. It wobbled a bit, especially when she reached the top, and for a moment she was sure she would fall. She remained perched on top for a while, crouched, with her hands gripping the little platform on top of the ladder, one foot on the rung just below it. When she felt she had regained her balance, she straightened up slowly.

Oh, but what a disappointment! The loft started at about Jiya's chin level. She could only reach with her

arms up to the bottom few books in the piles closest to her. She dared not risk pulling one of them out, for she'd only topple the pile. Bracing her arms on the loft, Jiya started to pull herself up. It was terribly difficult; she was annoyed how the children in the adventure stories she read managed to do this so easily.

Grunting from the effort, Jiya realised she would never pull this off. Her only hope was if she could free one arm and knock one of the books off the pile. She took a deep breath, and gave it all her strength. Heaving herself up, she reached for the closest pile and swiped as hard as she could. There was a flurry of dust and paper, and two of the thin notebooks fluttered down to the floor.

But before she could celebrate, she lost her balance and fell. One of her feet landed hard on the top of the ladder and the other missed it. But she had the presence of mind not to let go of the edge of the loft with her hand, and even as the ladder wobbled dangerously, Jiya hung on.

When her heart stopped feeling like it would burst out of her chest, she gingerly rested her full weight on top of the ladder. The next thing she knew was that she was sailing through the air. There was an almighty crash and for a few seconds Jiya lay on the floor, dazed.

When she realised she was miraculously unhurt, she also figured that Paati would have heard the commotion. She didn't stop to think. She scrambled up, grabbed the two dusty notebooks and fled. She took refuge behind the giant sofa in the living room, and opened the worn, yellowing pages just as she heard voices.

14 December 1976:
This was a completely forgettable experience. And a mistake. I must make a note to never ever target bathroom mirrors again. For one, it was horribly small and cramped, not to mention crowded. For another, and more annoyingly, each time someone came in—apart from myself, that is—I had to turn away.

Ick! Disgusting!

Suffice it to say, I didn't stay in this one very long. And I really don't want to talk about it.

The rest of the notebook was empty. It was an ordinary ruled notebook, similar to the kind Jiya used in school, but with only thirty or so pages in it. It had a thin faded cover with flowers printed on it, and the pages were now disintegrating with age. She turned to the other one. A similar notebook but with the picture of a girl.

8 October 1977:

Sometimes it can be quite a relief to get away. This time I watched the party from the confines of the antique mirror in the hall. And I don't use the term antique lightly. It is so old that the reflection isn't quite what it should be. It was such a relief to literally lie back, knowing that I didn't have to lift a finger to do anything. And yet, no one would miss me. Everyone would see me, greet me, smile at me. Tell me what a wonderful meal it was, and how nice the house looked. And I would smile and thank them ...

'Jiya!'

Jiya almost jumped out of her skin. Her grandmother looked down upon her from her not inconsiderable height, hands on her hips.

'Oh ... Paati ... I ...' stammered Jiya, getting to her feet.

'Are you hurt?' Paati interrupted.

'Um ... no.'

'You stupid girl!' cried Paati, lightly smacking the side of her head. 'You could have broken something. You could have been seriously hurt! The only reason I have you in the house by yourself is because I know you won't try anything silly. And now look what you've done!'

Jiya stared at the floor miserably.

'And what's that ... oh my god! Did you ... read?' Paati's voice rose in anger. 'I cannot stand disobedience. Did. You. Read?'

'I'm sorry,' whispered Jiya.

'You should be! I told you it was dangerous and that you were not to read my writing.'

'But it's just words, Paati,' said Jiya before she could stop herself. 'And I didn't really understand.'

Paati let out a long sigh like she was deflating. 'Oh Jiya, you ...' She shook her head. 'Come with me.'

She placed a hand on Jiya's shoulder and led her back to the bedroom. They sat side by side on the bed. Jiya hazarded a glance at her grandmother. She didn't seem angry any more, just a little thoughtful and sad.

'I ... I am really sorry,' said Jiya again.

Paati sighed again. 'It's all right. You didn't mean any harm.'

'You wrote about mirrors, but you don't like them. How come?'

Paati sat quietly for such a long time that Jiya thought she wouldn't answer.

'Each time we look into a mirror,' said Paati softly, 'we spawn a new self—you could say a copy of ourselves—a mirror-self—carved out of a little bit of our own soul. Every mirror we look into fractures us, little by little by little ... That is why some people go senile in their old age. They have looked into too many mirrors in their lifetime, and there's nothing left of them. And each of the mirror-selves, they remain trapped in their own mirrors. They can only go as far as the mirror can see. No further.'

'So you mean every mirror we've ever looked into has a bit of us inside?' asked Jiya incredulously. 'Like a copy of us? A clone?'

'Something like that, yes.'

'But then there must be so, so, so many people inside each mirror. Why can't we see them all?'

'Our mirror-selves only become visible when we ourselves are in its viewing range,' said Paati.

'Oh,' said Jiya, her mind racing. 'What happens to

mirrors in shops and things? There must be thousands of people inside them?'

A shiver wracked Paati. 'Yes. There are. Don't ask me. I can't bear to think about it.'

'But Paati, what about those notebooks? You wrote them all, right? There are hundreds of them. Are they all about mirrors?'

Paati sighed. 'Yes, they are. I wrote them when I ... after I ...'

Jiya waited impatiently.

'My children think that I am mad,' said Paati, suddenly changing the subject. To Jiya's alarm, a tear rolled down her cheek. 'They don't believe me.'

Jiya took the old woman's hand. It was wrinkly and spotted, but soft and warm. 'But I believe you, Paati.'

Paati squeezed her hand and smiled through her tears. 'Yes, I know that, and that's why I'm going to tell you, but will you promise me not to tell anyone?'

'I promise,' said Jiya solemnly.

'I know how to get inside mirrors,' was Paati's next surprising confession. Jiya's eyes went round, but her grandmother didn't stop. 'And when you enter a mirror, you free your mirror-self from there and take its place.

Each of those notebooks you saw contains an account of each time I entered a mirror.'

Jiya gasped. 'You mean you did it many times?'

Paati nodded. 'Four hundred and seventy-eight times. I let four hundred and seventy-seven mirror-selves of mine experience freedom for a short time.'

'How did you come out? If it's that easy to come out, wouldn't all our mirror-selves ... er ... escape?'

'Oh no,' said Paati. 'They don't have an anchor to the real world, you see. Me—I had your Thatha. He was the only one who didn't think I was insane. Each time I went into a mirror he said he would be waiting for me to come back, and each time I did ... I could.'

'But when Thatha died ...'

'I had nothing left to come back to,' finished Paati.

Jiya's heart was racing. 'You said four hundred and seventy-eight times, but four hundred and seventyseven mirror-selves. Does that mean ...'

Paati was nodding slowly. 'I am the four hundred and seventy-eighth.' She smiled, but this time Jiya didn't find the smile warm and loving.

'And I remain free.'

ALBATROSS

Kaushik Viswanath

Earthdate 30 February 2121

Alone.

You have no idea what aloneness is until you know this.

Help.

All I can do is scream the word and hope the laws of physics break so my voice will carry through the vacuum of outer space.

Stranded.

Most of the ship's systems have crashed. Communications are totally broken—there is no way I can get them working again. Navigation is down—the ship can't tell me where I am. I don't know how far the nearest space station or terraformed planet is. Shuttle supplies should last another two years.

Alone.

I have been alone since Earthdate 30 February 2115. Everyone else is dead.

Earthdate 30 February 2122

Today marks the seventh year I've been alone.

I used to make journal entries more frequently before. Now there's absolutely nothing to write. All my attempts to fix the shuttle's systems have been futile. All I do now is drift through space and hope some passing spaceship notices the *Albatross.*

But I know that's next to impossible. Even if a spaceship were passing nearby, without the *Albatross* transmitting some sort of signal, there's very little chance that I'd get noticed.

I sleep a lot these days. When I'm awake all I can hear is the deafening silence, but in my dreams ...

I have just one recurring dream, and technically it's a nightmare. But in this kind of aloneness and silence, a recurring nightmare can be ... well, it's better than nothing. At least it breaks the silence.

In my nightmare, I see the six other—dead—crew members of the *Albatross.* In my nightmare, they're alive, but they're screaming. They scream and scream and scream and beg for help and mercy until their throats and lungs can't scream anymore. And then they drop dead, one by one, all hitting the floor of the shuttle cabin with a dull thump. Their bulging dead eyes are all open and looking directly at me. Whatever it is that's killed them hasn't killed me. I move around, but their eyes seem to follow me.

And then I wake up.

There are seven sleeping pods on the *Albatross.* Six of them contain corpses. I've considered ending it all, putting a corpse in the seventh sleeping pod as well. Yet, somehow, in seven years, I haven't been able to commit suicide. I suppose I'm still clinging on to some unrealistic hope that I'll be rescued.

In any case, there's no point killing myself now. The *Albatross's* supplies will only last another year. After that, I'm dead anyway. I might as well wait.

Earthdate 21 March 2122

Voices.

I can't be sure, but I thought I heard voices. I definitely heard something. One does notice when a seven-year silence is broken. I heard a sound, and I woke up.

Now that I think about it, it's entirely possible that the sound I heard was in my dream. But then ... the screaming in my nightmares never wakes me up. This sounded like it came from the radio. I don't know. Now the sound is gone.

One part of me is almost certain that there was actually a sound, but considering what I think I heard, it's very likely that it was only in my dreams.

Because what I think I heard was human voices screaming.

And I think they were screaming *Help*.

Earthdate 02 April 2122

I haven't heard any sounds from the radio or anything else since 21 March. I'm now almost entirely certain that I didn't actually hear anything that day.

For the last few days I've been waiting to hear something more from the radio, just in case what I heard was real. But I haven't heard anything, and while that's a little disappointing, it's also slightly relieving. I mean, the last thing I need right now is somebody else screaming for help over the radio. *I* need to be rescued—I'm in no position to rescue anyone else.

Earthdate 17 May 2122

Static.

Almost two months since I heard—or thought I heard—the voices on the radio. Today I heard static. There's no doubt about it. I was fully awake when I heard it.

Four short bursts of white noise on the radio, about two minutes apart, each lasting about five seconds.

The first three times it sounded like pure static. Nothing but the plain *shshshsh* of white noise.

The fourth time there was something underneath the noise. I can't be sure, since it was so faint, but the fourth burst definitely sounded different from the first three. There was some other sound beneath the static.

Again, I can't be sure.

But I think I heard *music*.

Earthdate 31 May 2122

It's been driving me crazy. Nothing's come out of the radio since the static on 17 May. I keep fiddling with the knobs and the switches, but the radio remains silent. I don't care what the sound is—even if it's more static, I *need* to hear it.

I know there's nothing I can do. The radio's not going to generate noise on its own; it needs to pick up a signal. But that doesn't prevent me from continuously adjusting the controls. I'm desperate. I need to hear that sound again.

Tonight, before I lie down beside my six dead companions and dream that they're alive and dying, I'll pray.

Tonight I pray to the one white Teapot floating in space.

O benevolent Teapot, you've ignored all my prayers until now, but please answer my prayers tonight.

I'm not praying that I get rescued, since I've already prayed for that with no result.

I'm not praying that you fix the *Albatross*—you've shown you can't do that, either.

I'm not even praying that I hear a voice on the radio.

I'm praying for something really small, so you can't refuse me.

I'm praying that I hear static on the radio again. *That's all.*

Praise Tea.

Good night.

Earthdate 01 June 2122

I simply cannot believe it. I guess the Teapot answers small prayers after all.

Static.

Never have my ears heard a sweeter sound, never have I been so thrilled to hear such a meaningless noise. Continuous, uninterrupted static. It's been going on for about four hours.

It's not just static. In the last half hour or so, there have been variations in the noise—variations that make it seem like there's something underneath all the static. It's all very garbled and unintelligible, but sometimes there are brief snatches—lasting just a couple of seconds—where the sound gets slightly clearer. Even during these snatches the sounds are garbled, but the garbled sounds sound a lot like human voices. It's still very unintelligible, so I can't make out what the voices are saying.

If they are saying anything, that is.

It's entirely possible that the voices aren't saying anything. Although I hate to believe it, there is another possibility:

The voices are screaming.

And now the radio is silent again.

Earthdate 02 June 2122

The static lasted yesterday for about four hours. Towards the end of that period, I thought I heard voices talking ... or screaming. Then all sounds stopped, including the static.

The static came back just about an hour ago. For the first few minutes it was just the white noise. About ten minutes later there was a voice. A man's voice. This time it was much clearer than yesterday. There was someone on the other end trying to make contact. At first, I couldn't understand what he was trying to say, but the sound gradually got a little clearer.

'Hello?' he said. 'We are receiving signals from ... we don't know ...'

It didn't make much sense at first ... the man was talking about some signal flooding their communication systems.

'Please stop ... music's flooding channels ...'

From what I could make out, he seemed to think there was someone deliberately flooding their communication channels with this music.

A few seconds later, I could hear the music myself. It was getting steadily louder, as the man grew increasingly hysterical.

'What's going on ... please ... who's doing this?'

The music kept growing louder, and the man had to yell so his voice wouldn't be drowned out.

'Stop it! ... Whoever's doing this, please ...'

Then the music stopped, suddenly, abruptly. The man sighed.

'Thank you,' he said, feebly.

And then the yelling began. It wasn't the man, but voices in the background that were screaming.

'Oh god ... help ... please help ... SOMEBODY! THIS IS THE CREW OF CARGO SHIP TITUS ... WE'RE ... can't ...'

I sat by the radio, unable to do anything but listen. I couldn't even respond to the man over the radio.

Next their yells for help turned into high-pitched, hysterical screams. Loud, monosyllabic screams. The screams did not stop. Not one of the voices stopped to breathe. They were screaming until their lungs were drained, and then they screamed some more.

Then one by one the screams fell silent, and then I heard the gentle thump of the crew of Cargo Ship Titus, sinking to the floor, dead.

Then there was nothing. Not one sound.

Earthdate 03 June 2122

My nightmare was different last night. Usually I hear my shipmates screaming their lungs out in my nightmare. This time I couldn't hear it. This time I dreamt that my shipmates stood behind a sheet of glass. I stood on the other side. At first they yelled at me through the glass, confused, shocked. Then, gradually, they opened and closed their mouths, clutched at their throats, and began to gasp and choke. From where I was standing, it looked like they were screaming—only, I couldn't hear the screams through what seemed like a soundproof sheet of glass. Some of them banged against the sheet of glass, weakly, while the others grasped at invisible straws in the air as their popping eyes rolled upwards, revealing only whites. As the crew dropped dead, their pupils rolled down again. Their bodies, turned a pale blue from asphyxiation, lay lifelessly in different positions on the other side of the glass. And all their dead eyes remained open, staring. At me.

When I first got on board the *Albatross*, I was scared as hell of outer space. The sheer size, the scale of it, frightened me. The indomitable human mind can't begin to grapple with that kind of vastness. Space doesn't just dwarf humans, it renders us absolutely insignificant. If space tends towards infinity, everything within it tends towards nothingness. But what if space doesn't just *tend* towards infinity, what if it *is* infinity? In the face of infinity, everything is reduced to not just insignificance, but inexistence.

It also means that in the infinity of space, anything is possible. Anything that's imaginable or even unimaginable will exist in infinity, because small odds multiplied by infinity equal certainty. This means that somewhere out there, there's a planet that's made entirely out of chocolate, populated only by lonely, beautiful women. It also means that somewhere out there, there's some horrifying ... thing that announces its arrival with a signature theme song and causes spaceship crews to scream their lungs out and die.

At that time, I thought going into space would make me overcome my fears. After all, I was going on board with six highly trained, experienced cosmonauts. As an engineer, maintenance of the ship was my only responsibility. The others would handle the rest. What could go wrong?

What could go wrong.

I don't remember much from before the flight. Hurtling through the blackness of outer space makes you forget things. My life before the *Albatross* is like one of those dreams that you remember in full detail when you wake up, but gradually forget through the course of the day. My day is almost done, and that dream is almost entirely forgotten.

Even my memories of the actual flight are hazy. I can remember the last seven years quite clearly, but I can hardly recall what happened before that. I remember the years I've been alone only because there's not much to remember. After the crew died, every day has been a déjà vu of the previous one.

Except for these last few months, of course.

I could always look at the crew's logs to remind myself of what happened before, but I won't. I'm scared of what I might find. If I'm rescued, somebody will read the logs and tell me what happened, how the crew died. And if I'm not ... well, if I'm not rescued, what difference does it make?

Earthdate 10 June 2122

I'm saved.

Finally finally finally finally finally finally finally someone's found me.

Teapot bless you, *Rescue Ship Pangaea.*

After a week of silence, my radio crackled to life about half an hour ago. It was a rescue ship that had been sent to investigate the strange radio messages and distress signals that *Cargo Ship Titus* and others had transmitted over the last few months. They found the *Albatross.* I know all this because the captain of *Pangaea* stated his objectives over the radio. And what terrific luck—it's a rescue ship. No other ship would ever have bothered to approach a ship that wasn't responding to radio signals.

I hate to admit it, but there's a bit of me that's actually grateful for whatever it is that killed those other crews. If it weren't for that, a rescue ship would never have come this way.

The radio is crackling again.

'This is the captain of *Rescue Ship Pangaea* ...'

Oh captain of *Rescue Ship Pangaea*, how I love you. I would willingly be your slave for life. I will sing songs in your praise until the day I die. Thank you thank you thank you.

'... this is the captain of *Rescue Ship Pangaea* ... if there's anyone listening ... we've identified your ship as *Mining Ship Albatross* ...'

Mining Ship. I had completely forgotten that.

'... *Mining Ship Albatross*, we request you to kindly stop all radio transmissions temporarily ...'

What transmissions? I can't make any transmissions.

'... as our channels are being flooded ...'

Oh no. Not that dreaded tune.

'... with *music*.'

That same damned music.

Earthdate 11 June 2122

Rescue Ship Pangaea is dead. The captain and all its crew. Killed by the same thing that killed the crew of *Cargo Ship Titus* and god knows how many other ships.

And now I'm alone again. It won't be for long, though. It's only a matter of time before that thing finds me and kills me, as well.

I just hope it comes soon. I'm sick of waiting. And I'd much rather face this thing and be killed by it than have to slowly starve to death. I can forget about another rescue ship finding me. The odds of my finding that chocolate planet are better.

Earthdate 12 June 2122

I did not hope in vain. At this very moment, I can hear music softly leaking out of my radio. Although it's soft, it's somehow clearer than all the previous times I heard the music—this time I know I'm not hearing it from some other ship's radio. This time I know it's coming out of my radio directly.

The music grows louder, and it sounds vaguely familiar. Not because I've heard it so much over the past few weeks—it sounds more familiar than that—like I know it from long ago.

The music keeps growing louder.

I should be scared, but I'm actually rather relieved. This is it. This is the end of my seven-year agonising loneliness, the end of a completely pointless period of waiting. I suppose I'll get to see something new, something no other living person, I presume, has seen. Of course, I won't live to talk about it, but it beats not living to talk about slowly shrivelling up and rotting to death on board the *Albatross*.

The music is growing even louder. It's beginning to become painfully loud.

I've just noticed something wrong. I should have noticed this a long time ago. Oh my ... how did ... I don't ... understand how ... uh ...

All I can say is that ... this is very ...

Approximately seven years ago, six out of seven of the crew of the *Albatross* died. I was the only survivor. Snatches of memory are reappearing in my mind. One day they were alive, the next day they were dead.

I remember ... I remember having gone down to the engine room ... it was for routine maintenance. I was checking the ship's power systems ...

Something went wrong down there. I did something I shouldn't have done. I don't remember what exactly I did, or why I did it ... it could have been a mistake—negligence, or distraction, or maybe my hands fumbled.

Or maybe I had some inexplicable destructive urge.

Whatever the reason, I caused a power surge ... I remember ... on that day ... music playing on the ship's cabin speakers.

The music is really loud now.

I recognise this music. It's the same music that played on the deck of the *Albatross* that day seven years ago. Quiet, inoffensive music that, according to the captain, kept everyone in a good mood.

The music is now so loud it's turning into a violent noise. I fight with the radio controls, attempting to turn it off, turn down the volume, or retune it so it stops playing this.

The power surge that day made the speakers suddenly blare out the music at a high volume. The captain's quiet, inoffensive music was now loud, distorted, ugly, angry. It got loud enough for me to hear down in the control room. Then there was an explosion—in the engine room, because of the surge. It wasn't very large—the safety suit I was wearing managed to protect me from the blast, but the explosion had affected a lot of other systems. The lights immediately went out. The captain called my radio to ask what was going on. He said they'd been locked in the sleeping cabin. I turned on my torch and rushed back up to the deck to see what was going on. There were six of them, trapped behind the transparent door of the sleeping cabin. The door was meant to act as a security barrier—it was unbreakable. They tried opening the door, but it seemed like the door's systems had been affected by the explosion. The door refused to open. I broke open the electronic panel next to the door and tried to find a way to reopen it.

The captain said over the radio that it was getting very hot in there, and that the air felt heavy. We couldn't hear each other's voices across the door. I continued to struggle with the door's electronics, but it didn't look like I was making much progress.

I watched as the crew members' breathing started to get laboured and uncomfortable. The oxygen recycler. They weren't able to breathe because the oxygen recycler inside the sleeping cabin had also failed after the explosion, leaving them in an airtight space that was quickly running out of oxygen.

I kept struggling with the door. I watched them gulp and gasp for air on the other side. It looked like they were screaming. They began to claw at the door, and watched me with pleading eyes as they slowly slumped to the floor one by one.

I rushed back down to the engine room to see if I could fix anything. It took me a while to restore power to the door's system to get it open again. I ran back up, dreading what I'd find.

Six corpses lay on the floor of the sleeping cabin.

I eventually went back down, and was able to fix a number of the damaged systems. But the ship's navigation was damaged beyond repair and so was the ... communication.

The *Albatross's* communication systems had been completely destroyed. They haven't worked for the last seven years. I haven't been able to send out radio transmissions ... or receive any.

I've stopped fighting with the radio controls. The music has stopped.

Little Pig, Little Pig

Nilanjana S. Roy

It's when she's reaching up for the ball, on her toes, tendons stretched, that Anusuya knows for sure something's wrong. Her hand connects, and she knows that the ball will soar up, so close, but hit the rim of the basket instead of going all the way home.

What's bothering her is the scratchy feeling at the back of her throat, a soreness in her muscles, the sense that her body is being slowly squeezed to bits by a giant. She's already a star athlete; she's the only girl from Class V on the school team. But she struggles for the rest of the game with a growing sense of bonelessness and muscle ache.

'Not one of your best performances, Anu,' says Mr Pinto, her coach. There's no judgement in his voice, he's just surprised. She nods. 'I'm sorry, coach,' she says, standing up and reaching for her gym bag. Her head whirls and for the first time in her life, Anu faints. She's conscious of feeling cold, shivering, just before she hits the ground.

The voices swirl above her head. She feels as though she's under water, her face pressed up against something cool and green, listening from a great distance.

'... burning up ... shouldn't have been playing ...'

'... said nothing, I had no idea ...'

'... phoned her mother ... doctor ... should be here ...'

Then the world closes over her, and she floats off into the stillness.

Lemongrass and mothballs. The pillowcase seems to stretch on forever, an ocean of cool, clean, scented white. Someone's put a blanket over her but she wants to tell them it's the scratchy one, it needs a sheet beneath it. Someone's massaging her head with strong, capable fingers. Again, she has that sense of being underwater, the way she feels when she dives from the highest diving board and cuts into the water, the way she feels when she puts out a hand and touches the tiles on the floor of the pool, cocooned by the silence of the water.

She can hear voices. Doc Mukherjee's calm, rumbling tones. 'Malaria ... dangerously high fever ... these pills, four times a day ...'

She closes her eyes. Sleep envelops her like a heavy razai.

The room is filled with the insistently sweet scent of roses. They've been shoved clumsily into vases that occupy any free space, niches in the bookshelf, free space on the dressing table, the foot of the bed. Some are still cellophane-wrapped. A banner on the wall opposite that she can see if she raises her head a few painful inches says, 'Get Well Soon, Anusuya!!!!'

The words echo and shimmer in her mind. Get Well Soon Anusuya. Got Wall Scones Anusunya. Grit Hell Spoons Anaesthesia. It doesn't make sense. She's not well. How long has she been sick?

Someone's in the room. She turns her head, feeling the full leaden useless weight of it. She tries to speak, but it's tiring. She concentrates on getting the words out: 'How long have I been ill?'

The blurred outlines of a face swim into view. Her mother's small, worried features. At first Anu can't understand what she's saying, the words are dancing in her head. Doing the rumba, samba, salsa, tango and cha-cha-cha, with a bit of Bharatnatyam and Kathakali thrown in just for variety. If she tries really hard, she can understand maybe one word out of seven. 'Eed is phai summacks do squaps malaria and tentam pergo sansum all of us worried strak ferish nambla two weeks two weeks two weeks.'

It echoes in her head. Two weeks. Two weeks. Fourteen days. She can't work out how many hours. A million zillion hours? No, surely less than that. A few hundred hours? Must be more than that. Her sheets are soaked. Where did the last two weeks go? She wishes someone would change the sheets. Her mother is speaking, her mouth opening and closing. She looks like a fish. Anusuya tries to say, 'Ma, you look like a fish.' Her eyes close. She sleeps.

When she wakes up, it's night. The window is dark, there's just a bedside lamp winking solemnly in the blackness. Her room is cool and though her bones hurt, she feels better.

Her mother is sleeping in the shabby pink-striped chair right next to the bed. Anusuya reaches for a glass of water, not wanting to disturb her, but the movement wakes her up. She smiles at her daughter. 'Feeling any better, Anu?'

'A little. Ma, you've been here all through?'

'Yes, darling. You had a lot of fever this afternoon, but it seems to have gone down now. Do you want the TV on?'

Anu thinks about it. Then she smiles. 'Would you read me a story, Ma?'

It's one of their oldest rituals; the bedtime story. And her mother's face softens as she picks up a book of fairy tales; her voice is calm and soothing and those magic words, 'Once upon a time', lull Anu into a deep sleep.

That night, Anusuya dreams.

It starts well. She's playing basketball, and she's the captain of the team. They've been practising for months together, and they respond to each other's moves instinctively, seamlessly. She's laughing as she scores a basket, and then another; as she blocks an over-ambitious defender from the other team, and figures out their strategy, and sends in her people, in deadly knots of twos and threes, to dismantle their game plan. She's laughing as she stretches and leaps up and from an impossible but possible distance, scores the winning basket ...

... and she comes down, walking on air, and she lands in the middle of a forest, a thicket of thorn trees and deodars and she looks around for her team, but they're gone, sucked somewhere else in the middle of this deep green hilly silence, and there's just her, in her basketball shift.

She's tired, and sweaty. There's a clearing ahead, with a teeny-tiny cottage in the middle of it, and nothing has ever looked that inviting, and she walks towards it. And oh. And oh, because inside, it's just as cozy as it seems. There are clean clothes laid out—for her? Well, they're in her size—on the dining table, and she finds herself walking upstairs, to the shower, which is blessedly, beautifully, perfectly warm. She showers, she dresses, she comes downstairs and rests in the chaise lounge that curves lovingly round her body, and she drifts off to sleep.

It's the knocking at the door that wakes her, a thunderous clang-clang-clang that shifts her out of the dream sleep. 'Who's there?' she calls.

And a voice as deadly as datura and as pleasant as marshmallow says, 'It's me, it's the big bad wolf. Little pig, little pig, let me come in?'

In her dream, she is feisty. She calls back, 'You're not getting in; not by the hair of my chinny-chin-chin.' And she settles back, drawing her hands in ... trotters, they're trotters, and her nose/snout is whiffling overtime, and her pink skin has hairs standing up on end, and she is grunting, and looking up at the ceiling, which is made of straw, and somehow, she knows she has to run, NOW, and she leaps out of the chair on all fours ... The door opens at the pressure of her snout, but as she trots, she smells something dank and feral, something so wild that her porcine nostrils go crazy. She smells predator, and blood, and she sees those intelligent wolf's eyes, roaming and fixing on her ... and she squeals, and runs for what her life is worth ...

Those teeth flash down just behind her hooves; she kicks up mud in a panic to blind the predator. Ahead, she just knows it, is a house made of wood and twigs, if only she can reach that; but the wolf's teeth snap on air, and then snap again, and she feels a searing pain in the tendon on her left foot. She turns, panicked, and looks

right into the maw of the wolf, its leering, saliva-specked tongue, its sharp, unforgiving teeth, its red throat—and she squeals again, despairingly, as the teeth fasten on her neck.

And then she wakes up. Her mother is bustling around the room. Anusuya has been changed, she is in fresh clothes, and her skin smells less stale—she has been sponged. The bedclothes smell of lemon and lavender, and the flowers have been renewed—fresh bouquets litter the end of the bed.

'Ma,' says Anusuya, 'did you get any sleep?'

Her mother turns, and smiles. Her face looks drawn and tired, but her eyes are as twinkly as ever. 'You had a rough night, baby,' she says, 'it's the fever dreams—that can happen with malaria.'

Anusuya frowns. 'They seemed so real,' she says, 'kind of scary.'

Her mother nods. 'Once your fever comes down, the dreams will go. They're only dreams, baby. I'll get you some breakfast—something light, all right?'

Anusuya nods as her mother shuts the door behind her. She burrows back under the sheets, and something scratches her lightly—a thin, thorny twig. She looks at it, puzzled, and then looks around at the flowers that some of her friends and teachers have been sending. It must have fallen out from one of the bouquets, she thinks, closing her eyes.

She drifts in and out of sleep that day, but whenever she wakes up, she finds her mother there, her mother's hands, smelling of Johnson's Baby Lotion and haldi-and-garlic, gently smoothening her brow.

The next day is much, much better. Some of her friends come over—Sameera, the awe-inspiring games captain, Shahana, the giggly friend who shares the back bench with her, three of her team mates. She's happy to see them, but she tires quickly, unable to sustain the conversation for more than fifteen minutes. They leave, their voices echoing cheerfully around the room:

'See you at the St Ignatius versus Columbus game!'

'I'll bring you some comic books, okay? The new Sandman's just come in ...'

'We'll have a party on Facebook when you're feeling better, Anu.'

She falls back into sleep the moment they've left. She's in a house, deep in the heart of the forest. It's made of twigs and wood, and it smells of fresh-cut trees. She likes it here. There's a small cluster of apples and nuts scattered on the mud floor, and she gets down on all fours, snorting and grunting, and snuffles after them.

'The doctor's coming,' her mother's voice says, far, far away. 'Let's get you dressed.'

She eats an apple, and it tastes of the sun and of summer. She stretches, and her skin feels loose and beautiful; it's a shade of pink she's never seen before, the blood coursing beneath the veins. She trots away from the apples and finds a beautiful bed of warm, comforting mud; she digs herself in and wallows to her heart's content.

There's the cold sting of the stethoscope on her chest. 'Breathe in,' says Dr Mukherjee. 'All well, my dear?'

She has to shake herself out of that clean, comfortable pink pig's skin; she has to work hard to come back into her long athlete girl's body. She starts to tell him about her dreams, about the wolf knocking at the door, but a drowsiness overtakes her. 'That's not good,' she hears. '104 at this stage is unusual, I'd better stay.'

She slips back into sleep, and now she's at the bottom of a ravine. There's a waterfall nearby, but she's pressed down, her belly close to the moss. She is quivering with fear. She doesn't know how she knows this, but her pink skin is drenched with sweat, her nose is twitching in distress: she is the prey. Far away in the corners of her mind, a voice tells her to be strong, to leap and run like the basketball player, to trust to her sinews and tendons, to turn and face the predator. But she cannot do this.

The wolf lopes into view, handsome and sleek, at the top of the hill. She prays that it cannot smell her, cannot smell the sweat and the fear coming off her.

'An injection might help,' says Dr Mukherjee's voice, far away. 'I've never seen a case like this, Mrs Banerji. Quite inexplicable.'

If she breaks cover and runs like the wind, she might find her way to a cottage built of twigs and wood. She might. But if she stays still, perhaps the wolf won't notice her.

'You'll need more of those cold cloths, Mrs Banerji,' says Dr Mukherjee. 'We have to get her temperature down.'

Ice bands her forehead, and somehow, she knows. The wolf hasn't changed position; it stays up there, silent, beautiful and deadly in silhouette. But she knows and it knows. It has her scent. It knows where she is.

'Metakalfin. It's the wonder drug of this decade, Mrs Banerji. If anything can help your daughter now, it's this.'

She breaks. She can feel the power in her hind legs, the desperation that drives her forward. She can sense the wolf turning, its eyes narrowing joyfully as it marks its prey. She has to make it to the cottage. She must. There is no other way.

'No! Don't let her thrash around so much! She must have the injection, and if the needle breaks off ...'

She can feel its breath, rank and feral, thick with the blood of its last kill, on her shoulders. And just as she's about to give up, there it is: the cottage. She sobs as she runs through the door. She is safe here, for now.

Little pig, says the voice in her head. It is sad and sorrowing, hopeful and despairing. Little pig, little pig, let me come in?

She gulps. Perhaps it's reformed, she thinks, and then she looks at the thin bleeding gash on her flank. Perhaps not.

Not by the hair of my chinny chin chin.

Then I'll huff and I'll puff and I'll blow your house down.

'Anu,' says her mother, 'Oh, my Anusuya.'

She rolls thankfully into her mother's warmth, her embrace. The shots have taken their effect. There is no warm, rank wolf-breath; she is not a pig, just a young girl suffering from malaria. Dr Mukherjee's face, bespectacled, swims into view, and she smiles at him.

'You had a few bad moments there, my dear,' he says.

'I know,' she says, 'but I guess it'll be fine now. It must have been the fever.'

'Yes,' he says, 'malaria can do strange things.'

She rests, looking up at the whitewashed ceiling, down at the brocaded curtains, around at the quiet normalcy of her room. She feels a slight itch, and massages a small scratch on her leg—she must have cut herself somehow, thrashing around with the fever.

But it will be all right; in a week or two, she'll be back at the basketball courts, perhaps a little weaker than normal. She'll get her strength back eventually, and she can still be there for the big game, the one versus Loyola.

She can hear the front door open and close, as her mother goes out to see off Dr Mukherjee. Her bedroom window opens out onto the road, and she can hear their voices, a distant, comforting murmur.

Anu wonders whether she should switch on the TV, but the remote control is out of reach, and she doesn't feel like getting up. The pillows have been stacked just right; she likes their coolness against her head.

Then she hears a creak, as the front door opens again. That must be Ma, coming back in; but no, her mother is still outside, talking to the doctor.

The bedroom door opens just a crack. She can see the red reflection from the Chinese lantern in the hallway. 'Ma,' calls Anusuya. 'Ma, is that you?'

There is no response, but she can hear something now. It sounds like the heavy breathing of a dog, she thinks, except that she doesn't know anyone who has a dog in the neighbourhood. There's a strange smell. Like wet fur and the rotting leaves in a forest.

'Ma?' calls Anu, but what comes out is a thin, high squeal. She turns, trying to get out of bed, and feels a heavy, hairy paw across her windpipe, and looks into a pair of flat yellow eyes. The wolf's muzzle is matted and its breath stinks of rotting meat. There is mud on the sheets, and at the bottom of the bed, her flailing feet catch on thorny branches.

Outside, her mother is saying, 'I hope so, doctor. I'll try the lemon barley water, she hasn't been able to keep much down.'

Inside Anu's room, as her bones are snapped one by one, a voice, as deadly as datura and as soft as marshmallow, says softly, 'Hello, pig.' And then the wolf's gleaming white teeth flash down.

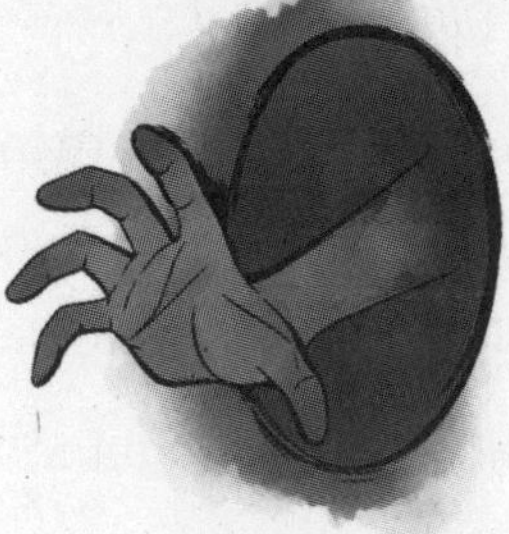

IT HAPPENED THAT NIGHT

Arunava Sinha

When ma said we were invited to Toni Mashi's, I had no idea things were going to change forever. I didn't even want to go. Even today, I don't know whether not going would have made things any different. It was just a week before my fourteenth birthday. Baba and ma were, of course, not going to let me have a proper party. It's for the family, they said, in the same shiny tone they use when they're trying to make me do something I don't want to. I know the truth—

they don't want boys and girls partying in their house. Hypocrites. Like they didn't do this stuff.

So anyway, there we were, arriving after everyone else, as usual. Toni Mashi's daughter, Dahlia, was busy with her friends, so I couldn't talk to her though I wanted to. That left me with nothing to do because there was no one to talk to. Ma and baba were being their usual selves—ignoring me. I was trying to look sulky. The grown-ups were everywhere, behaving like they were 20 years younger than they are. Really, don't they know how silly they sound talking like us! And Facebook! That's all they can talk about!

I was standing at a window, looking down over the city—we were in a 23rd floor penthouse. Suddenly the lights went out, and everything became still. Very still. I held my breath. And nearly screamed. Something—or someone—was brushing against my leg. But then I remembered where I was so I sort of swallowed hard and looked down, though, who knows what you might discover if you look? And suddenly, in the pitch darkness, I felt this cold—no, icy—gust of wind hit my face. It was March! Where'd they get a cold wind like that? Anyway, they got the generator going a moment later and turned out that a waiter trying to offer me a glass of wine had stumbled in the sudden darkness and brushed past me. Ma or baba—whoever saw me first—would so kill me if I took one, though I was dying to.

I had to pick a piece of kabab instead. Blech. Suddenly I heard someone ask, 'Not into kababs, young man?'

Adult-trying-to-be-friendly alarms went off in my head instantly. But I could be rude only if I could get away with it. What if this guy was ma's friend? Or, worse, baba's? Baba would start his did-we-bring-you-up-to song immediately—and he can't even sing. Actually I'm not too sure what he can do, besides earning s***loads of money, give him that. All of which keeps us cool in summer and well fed in winter. Anyway. Back to the guy.

He's intent on conversation.

'So, dude, what kinda (not kind of, kinda) food you into?'

'I'm not into food, jerk, food's into me.'

That comes out as: 'Oh, whatever.'

'So, you have a Xbox, what's your favourite game on it?'

Before I know it, he's off on Xbox versus Wii. What's going on here? And why does this guy look kind of familiar anyway? As he kept asking me questions, I kept retreating, till I had my back to the wall and couldn't go any further. The last thing I remember before feeling this shock of recognition was him asking, 'And what do you think of the new U2 album?' I couldn't answer. I'd just realised he spoke exactly like my father did. Shut your eyes and it was baba all the way. Ewww!

Ma called me from somewhere. Her voice sounded funny, unnaturally loud. She never spoke so loudly. I just walked away to find her—wondering how I could hear her if I couldn't see her. The lights were flickering. The icy gusts were back. I couldn't recognise Toni Mashi's house anymore, though I'd been there a hundred times. Where were Dahlia and her friends? Where was everyone? I lurched out onto the terrace where everyone had been hanging out ... and walked straight into a blinding glare of light. Where was it coming from? I could see people, but had no idea who they were. They were all dark figures, feinting and bobbing. Where were ma and baba? Or for that matter all the mashis and uncles (they never liked to be called mesho)? Who were all these people? Sometimes there were tunnels in the glare I could see clearly through—there, wasn't that ma? But she was

gone as suddenly. I had a sharp feeling in my throat, like something was trying to force itself out. There was music from somewhere, was someone playing it out loud? What was that strange smell?

I have no idea what happened for some time after that. Suddenly, though, it ended—just as suddenly as it had begun. The bright lights were gone, the cold wind had gone, the smell was gone, everything was back to normal. I ran to baba, couldn't find ma anywhere. Then I was embarrassed, because he turned to me and behaved like w.e.i.r.d.l.y. He actually put his arm around my shoulder and said, 'Are you ok, Papu?' (That nickname—don't ask!) Gross! I'd never known him to do that. It would have been normal for him to just turn to me in irritation and say, 'Not now.'

I just shrugged his arm off and said, 'Where's ma?' Pointing to the far end of the terrace, he said, 'She was looking for you, too. Go talk to her.' I didn't really want to, but something made me walk over anyway. I still had this sense of unease, which was to be proved so right.

But not right then. Much later. In the car on our way back. Actually it started in the lift on the way downstairs. Normally ma and baba make these journeys in silence, yawning their heads off. This time, though, they were talking—in stiff, careful sentences. I'd never heard them that way with each other.

'Did you enjoy the food?'

'Not really, though the dessert was great. You?'

'It was all right.'

I mean, they were like people who'd known each other for a few hours. Small talk. Not my parents who had been, after all, living with each other for even longer than fourteen years—and boy, that's long! So why were they talking like that?

There were other funny things, too. Baba usually walks on ahead with his head down, rather fast. I didn't even try to keep pace the few times we went anywhere together. But now he was looking around, trying to walk out together. And ma was trotting up to him—she never did that either. What was going on? Had they had something strange to drink? For a wild moment I even wondered if they had tried some drugs or something—I know my parents and their friends used to be into all that. But with us, of course—as I said, hypocrites!

It got worse in the car. Now they were asking me questions—questions I'd never heard before. Not from them, anyway. Baba drove and ma was in the other seat, while I was pretending to sleep but couldn't. Something was eating away inside me. Every time the bright lights of the overhead metro lines cast a glow inside the car, I could see their faces in three quarter profile. Dude, they were so not my parents—not the ones I knew. They looked the same, but by the time the journey home was over, I was convinced these were other people in there.

The way they chatted with each other! Polite, like they didn't know each other. And baba's questions—endless questions—for me. What was I reading these days? Did I have any new friends? What was I thinking in terms of higher studies? All this at two in the morning! Suddenly the cold wind was back, this time enveloping me totally. Something had happened back there at Toni Mashi's place. Something awful. I think the people all got changed. And this guy ... this guy ... he wasn't my father, he was the guy who had been asking me funny questions earlier.

I knew with cold certainty it was the truth. To check, I asked ma if I could skip school on Monday as I wanted to watch a movie which was only being screened at eleven in the morning. You know what kind of an answer that would get, right? But not this time. She actually asked baba, 'Can we let him watch it? He's just finished his exams.' OK, so she may have said this if she was feeling especially mellow, but no way was baba going to agree. And, of course, he did!

Now I knew it. And I didn't know how to get away. What were they going to do to me? I was scared. I started sending an SMS to Dahlia, telling her to get her parents to visit us because I was sick, or ma was sick, whatever ... till I realised her parents may have changed, too. Something had definitely swirled things around in that mist ...

Back home, I escaped quickly to my room. When I awoke, there was no one at home. That was normal—they'd left for their offices. And since I had got permission to skip school, I was allowed to sleep in late. I wondered if it had all just been a bad dream ...

... and got the biggest scare of my life when baba ambushed me in the kitchen with a belly laugh. Baba laughing like that! But, of course, it wasn't him. Nor was it ma who joined us, laughing like I'd never heard her laugh. And the two of them said I was going to get a special drink they'd make for me—of course, baba couldn't stop himself from asking whether I preferred mango to watermelon and which of them I'd liked as a kid. Neither of them then, and definitely neither of them now. But what was I to do? There they were, the two of them, grinning at me, ma running the water, baba bearing down on me with a glass, promising me a drink, a drink, a drink ...

I had to stop thinking of them as ma and baba, of course. These were other people in there—put in there somehow.

But why did they want me to have that drink? What had they put in it? What was it going to do to me? Blind panic was flowing through me now. My feet were frozen. I couldn't run away. Baba—no, that man—was blocking the door anyway. He was coming towards me, glass in hand. And then, oh, wow, he skidded on the water leaking from the huge decanter on the shelf and, in trying to stop himself from falling, dropped the glass, which smashed on the floor.

'What do you want?' ma whispered. She never whispered. 'To meet Dahlia,' I said, without having the faintest idea why.

'He wants to meet Dahlia. Let's take him,' ma told baba. 'Now?' he asked. 'No, tonight,' she said. Both of them smiled and left the kitchen. I bolted. Out through the front door, ran all the way to Bubu's house. Bubu, my friend from the neighbourhood who never went to school, who ma and baba didn't know about.

I spent the day there before returning home in the evening. My heart was now throbbing like one of those generators late on a summer night during a power-cut. And I was sweating just like there WAS a real power-cut. But I knew I had to make that journey back to Toni Mashi's house, to find out how to fix this horrible mistake.

Baba and ma were all dressed for the visit. They looked like they had been expecting me to return any moment. They obviously knew. This time, on the way out, we didn't speak much. Baba drove very fast, weaving in and out of the traffic in a way I'd never seen him do. Ma kept looking back at me and smiling, smiles that almost reassured me. For a wild moment, I even thought, what's wrong with this? These people could be nice parents—they let me do as I please.

Just one moment, of course. I wanted my ma and baba, no one else. Strict, curt, unforgiving—but I wanted them.

We were about to reach Toni Mashi's. I wondered what the official reason for us to be there was. No idea.

Didn't care much either. As we went up in the lift, I only wondered who knew the secret—was it Toni Mashi? Her husband? Dahlia didn't, I was sure.

Baba rang the bell. Ma stood by him. I was behind them. The door opened. Baba and ma stepped aside. I saw Toni Mashi. She smiled at me. That same smile. 'Look who's here. Little Papu,' she said.

I tried to turn and run, but a force took hold of me and made me enter. I dimly sensed baba and ma behind me. I had no control over my feet. They just made me walk out to the terrace. And as I walked, I felt that icy wind sear my face. The mist. This time, nobody there. That smell.

I remembered it all. And then the mist lifted. I turned and walked back towards baba and ma. They smiled. I smiled. I wasn't afraid, though they were not my real baba and ma.

After all, I wasn't Papu anymore either.

MONSTERS ABOVE YOUR BED

Anshumani Ruddra

You pop your head through the wall and look around. There is no one in the room. Cautiously you glide in and head towards the table at the far end. You search frantically. It's there!

'Ink.'

Now you just have to hope that nature cooperates. It does. A strong wind comes in through the window blowing aside the curtains that knock over the brush stand and topple the bottle of ink to the floor.

'Score!'

You laugh nervously. There is ink on the floor, red ink. But your kind is colour blind—everything is in black and white. A broken brush floats in the air. It's an ability you have acquired recently. You make the brush dip itself into the pool of ink. And start scribbling on the white walls of the room.

Monster,

Greetings from the land of the dead and un-alive!

In a recent counselling session with Dr Prate, a leading psychiatrist and specialist in sub-normal phenomenon, I was advised to face my fears head on. Hence, this letter.

You move away from the wall to look at what you have written so far. Writing is new to you. You learnt it from the merry lot at the graveyard. Clean deft strokes, proper spacing, no smudges. Boo will be so proud.

Boo ... your friend.

The Monster had written some disparaging things about her in his diary. 'Lies! All lies! A sweet little banshee like her could never do something so despicable. Now, where is that diary?' You spot it on the corner of the table.

The pages flutter as you try and find the right one. There it is, with its inflammatory accusations. You read it just to fuel your anger and calm your wavering aura.

Boo!

She lives in a keyhole.

No key exists.

There is no danger.

She sits there. Looks. Toilet on one side. Bedroom on the other.

One day a thief comes by. He's foolish.

Doesn't know it's a toilet. Doesn't know it's unlocked.

Searches for wires. Finds one. Long. Thin.

Something is stuck inside.

Puts lips to the keyhole. Takes a deep breath.

Blows.

She is thrown out.

She is angry. Very.

He opens the door. Walks in.

And that is the gruesome end of his story.

'Preposterous! Boo wasn't angry. She was just frightened. And she wasn't thrown out. She was sucked in. There she was relaxing in the keyhole one day when someone started poking around with an iron wire!' You remember that banshees don't like iron. It interferes with their anthropomorphic field. Her field dissolved for the briefest of moments and suddenly she was being sucked into a vortex.

You shake your head. 'This thief, this human monster sucked Boo into his body!' You shudder when you think of the H word. 'There was no way she could just pass through him. Pass through like every other ... uggh ... solid object.' You know the rule well—if a monster invites you in, you cannot leave without his permission.

Poor Boo. She screamed and wailed. The thief monster was going crazy—slamming his body into the walls of the toilet, dipping his head into the commode, screaming angrily, 'There's something inside me ... inside me! Get out! OUT!!'

Permission. To. Leave.

So Boo got out, and there sprawled on the floor was the thief monster, dark blood oozing out of his wounds—all of them self-inflicted. 'How was this Boo's fault?'

Boo flew straight to the graveyard and didn't step out for months. 'These wretched monsters!' You dip the brush into the ink and start writing again with a renewed ferocity.

Sir, it has been brought to my attention that you have been writing incendiary accounts about my community, accounts that in the long run will breed distrust and malevolence towards us. And even though I would

be mortified to have a direct conversation with you, I propose that we meet at a time and place agreeable to you to address my community's grievances and dispel any wrong notions you may have about us.

Your most humble servant,

Gaayab

P.S. Please clean the floor under your bed once in a while.

A series of unfortunate events had led Premshankar Upadhyaya to become a thief, albeit not a good one. Not predisposed to being dextrous and instinctive, he had a tough time coming to terms with his profession. It also didn't help that he had the worst luck South of the Equator and North of the Tropic of Cancer. (Another, equally unlucky soul, resided between these two latitudes.)

And regular encounters of the paranormal variety didn't embellish his sparse resume either.

In the last incident, where he was possessed by what can only be described as a ghost, he broke his collar bone, three ribs and seven fingers and caused irreparable damage to several muscle tissues while trying to exorcise himself. He was subsequently arrested and served six months in prison.

Today the victim returns to the scene of crime; for what transpired on that dark and dreary night six months ago, was indeed a heinous and brutal crime—against him. As he steps in through the open window a chill runs down his spine. 'Something is wroo ... ong here,' his below par instincts tell him. His eyes take in the mess on the table and floor. 'Is that blood?' He almost jumps out of his skin. Then better sense prevails and he repossesses his epidermal cells. 'It's just ink, red ink,' he calmingly replies to his instincts. 'No need to get all jumpy now.'

He looks at the toilet door on his left and flinches. He breathes out, turns to his right, looks at the scribbling on the wall and takes in a deep breath.

There is a sudden chill in the air around him. He can feel his insides slowly freeze. 'No! Not again!' he

screams, clutching his hair with his fingers. 'Something ... is ... inside me.'

He really has the worst luck South of the Equator and North of the Tropic of Cancer.

Dear Diary,

Strange thing happened today. The thief who had turned up a few months back made another surprise visit. I found him passed out on the floor, red ink all around him. When the police shook him back to semi-consciousness he started babbling something about having been possessed by a ghost. Again! His two front teeth were missing, left shoulder dislocated and he was convinced that for a while he was floating a few inches above the ground.

He had thrown a few things around and written some rubbish on the wall. I think the poor man needs immediate medical help to untangle the mess that is in his head. I'll have to get someone to paint the wall tomorrow.

The scribbling on the wall is in the form of a letter, a letter written by a ghost. Could make for an interesting story. Imagine having monsters living under my bed, that want me to keep the floor clean. And want to meet me at a convenient time and place. How inspired!

So how would the story begin?

You pop your head through the wall and look around. There is no one in the room. Cautiously you glide in and head towards the table on the far end. You search frantically. It's there!

THE VOICE

Tanvi Mehta

I wake up with a headache that won't go away. Trying to ignore it, I go about getting ready as usual—but my body just feels unfamiliar. Standing in front of the mirror to brush my teeth, I raise my toothbrush up to my mouth—and miss it completely. *I don't remember my mouth being that high.* Or at least my hand doesn't. Maybe I slept in a bad position and my arm is just stiff. Shrugging, I get dressed—*my pants seem a bit too long, my shirt too roomy*—and head out the door, reaching for a granola bar on the way. Something feels odd.

I haven't slept very well; everything seems like a dream to me. Eyes, far too big for faces, beam at me disconcertingly. Movements seem unnaturally glitchy almost. Voices are just a little bit off pitch. I walk—stumble?—through my day, because coffee does nothing for me. The world just has an uncomfortable film over it.

Everything is far too quiet when I get home. I notice it immediately. I can suddenly hear my footsteps echoing through the house, getting louder and louder inside my mind, an uneasy, fearful feeling rising in my gut—inexplicable. I can feel the silence on my face, pressing gently, my skin tingling. Why does everything feel so odd?

Someone is following me. No. Nobody behind, nobody in any of the rooms. No shadows in the mirrors, no people in the dark corners. I check everything. What is it then, what's making the hair on the back of my neck stand? What is that eerie tickle I feel on my back, like someone is watching me? I can't shake off the feeling that *something is wrong.*

I sit down and turn on the TV, trying to dose off, drown out the white noise in my ears, but somehow I'm hyper aware of everything suddenly. My eyes dart around the room—and then I realise what it is. *The room seems smaller. My furniture is closer together.* I could've sworn there was at least two feet between the couch and the coffee table, but now they're almost touching. I blink—*and it's back to normal.*

Unsettled and undeniably uncomfortable, I decide to sleep off this strange state of mind. I get into bed—*and I can swear the room moves around me.* In immediate response, my bookshelf creaks just slightly, as if the weight it put on the wall is now on its legs. I have to believe this is in my head. I flip the light switch, and my hand drops down. There is a foot between the shelf and the wall. I don't know what to do. I sit and stare at the new space in petrified silence—what is happening to me?

I'm sure I'm imagining it. Furniture doesn't move. Walls don't either. *But why is there a space? Why can I see it?* I walk over and slip behind the bookshelf. An unearthly cold fills the space, and I can feel the goosebumps rise all over me. I don't know what else to do, so I go back to bed.

Somehow I feel more comfortable with the lights off. I lie there, silent and unmoving, unsure of what to do, staring at the ceiling. And then I hear it. At first, it's soft, almost non-existent, but then it gets louder,

echoing through the house—a woman's cry, broken and miserable, getting shriller and shriller until she is wailing—a blood-curdling, endless shriek. I follow the noise to its origin—*the wall.* Terror grips my throat. Something is in my house. Something is moving my walls, and there is nothing I can do about it. All I can do is watch the darkness, watch my walls, knowing that they're moving. I'm powerless. I could leave—but can I? I can't possibly walk through this abyss. I stare for hours at the dark space behind my bookshelf, until I slump back against the wall, asleep.

In the morning, I force myself to leave, to continue normally. My mind whirs endlessly; days pass uneventfully after this, but I can't focus on them anymore. I can't do anything. I go through the motions of my routine mindlessly, constantly glancing at the walls, making sure they're in the same place as they were a minute ago. Nothing new happens, but I'm paranoid—the thought has infested my mind, burrowing, making a home inside the pit of my brain, nestling comfortably, refusing to move. And then it happens again, just as I'm beginning to forget.

I'm in bed, staring at the walls blankly, when my bed groans, just slightly, but enough to be heard in the silence. I'm awake immediately. Lights on, I look around, almost reluctant to see what the movement was. I know before I see it. *There is a space right behind my bed.* The back wall has moved. I'm stiff, stuck to the bed, unable to do anything but turn off the lights and lie down, nerves on end, almost anticipating something, anything—but nothing happens. I'm useless against whatever this is—all I can do is wait for this *thing* to close in on me, soundless, just out of sight, but moving. I know it's there, I can almost feel it stroking my neck, right at the jugular with its nails—or are they teeth—teasing me. I can hear its silent laugh, and I know I should be running, or flinching at least, but I can't do anything, not even shiver at its touch, this unknown, unearthly creature. I spend the whole night waiting—but nothing happens. I sit, watching my walls, now home to this creature, the breath and blood pulsating in the life behind them, in this thing that sits somewhere in the dark, watching me like I watch the walls —only *amused* at me.

Morning comes—and with light comes sleep. In the light, I know somehow that it can't do anything—walls don't move in the day. I wake up hours later with a start—plates are crashing in the kitchen and I have a sinking feeling about it. Sure enough, something is wrong. Very wrong. The entire cupboard of plates is missing, with only a blank wall in its place. The plates continue to crash *behind the wall* for a minute—and then silence.

I've had enough. I force myself to leave the house. Outside feels safe, good almost. I take a long, forcedly relaxed walk around the mall, stopping at the electronics store to pick up the highest quality video cameras I can afford. Then I get food—I've barely eaten in days, I realise, and sit at my table, deciding to stay until I'm asked to leave, because I know if I go outside *It* will tempt me back, pull at my curiosity, slip its nails under my skin and tug just slightly, and I will have to go back.

Eventually, I head home. I set up the cameras in each room—if something is moving my walls I'd like to see it. Then, I measure. I spend hours drawing out a detailed plan of the house, marking every dimension carefully, measuring each length again and again until I've convinced myself—until I've convinced *It*—that I'm sure. The plates are back, unbroken, inside their cupboard, which has reappeared somehow. *What is happening to me?*

After I'm done, I sit aimlessly, unable to do anything but watch the walls, wait for something to happen, for *It* to show itself, because I know it's there, behind my walls, watching me, laughing at my futile efforts to track *It*, to see what its plan is for me, for this house. *It* knows I'm useless, that nothing I do will help me, that I'm so stupid, so stupid for even trying. Not even the TV will drown out the white noise anymore, so I just wait for *It* to show itself somewhere, in some wall or shelf—because what else can I do? I'm resigned to simply sitting here, attending to *Its* twisted smile, its unearthly scream, so high-pitched and unnatural that it's only in my head that I can hear it. I can't leave this house, not for anything, because what would *It* do without me? It thrives off me, it lives off my very existence, and without me, who will show the world what *It* is?

Hours pass. Nothing has moved. I'm beginning to get impatient, so I check. I measure every length, every corner. I walk past every shelf, looking, desperately for change. I pace around and around the house, one shoulder dragging against the wall—leaning, but still moving, staring at the floor—what if that moves and suddenly there's just empty space below me? I listen to the walls, one ear pressed against the painted smoothness, under which I know lives a living, breathing being, and I can hear the voices, the whispers and moans, the *cries* of the people it's seen and laughed at—because I can't be the only one—the ones it's crept up behind and slowly but deliberately sucked the life out of through the mind—and I'm lying on the floor now, dragging myself, because I need to be touching as much of the house as I can, I need to *feel Its* presence, and lying down allows me that—greater surface area, you see, and I strain my ears to hear that soft cry that tells me that It is back—knowing where *It* is makes me feel better I think.

And then the screaming is back, and it's filling my head, filling my nerves, and numbing my senses so I won't feel *It* coming when it does. I keep crawling, keep trying to follow the sound that's moving around so fast all of a sudden—and then I'm scratching at the walls, trying to find It, needing to see It. I take a knife from the kitchen and start hacking at my walls, and suddenly they're all moving, the whole house is changing shape and all that stays constant is the wall I'm attacking—and I see it, empty eyes staring at me, a demonic smile twisting whatever face it has, bony hands reaching for me, leaving dark red scratches across my skin as the panic sets in and I try to fight back. I can't breathe, its face leaning in, closer and closer, until I can feel its breath on my neck, its nails drawing blood across my face. Wordlessly, It pulls me into its hole, into the cold, swampy darkness behind the walls, and all I can hear is the screaming inside my head, inside Its head, as everything goes black.

I wake up in agony, on the floor next to the wall. Stiff and in pain, I get up and look at myself in the mirror—and my stomach drops. Cuts adorn my face—but they are clean and precise. *I have been cut only by a knife.*

The wall is untouched. *The bookshelf has been pushed forward.* Only the bloody knife with my blood all over it lies on the floor where I woke up.

SHAKTI

Nalini Ramchandran

'How? How? How?!' Anya grumbled as she stormed into her house.

Her mother watched quietly as the 14-year-old flung her school bag across the room.

'Did you have a tiff with your new school friends again?' she asked Anya. Anya didn't respond. 'Do you want to talk about what happened?' her mother tried once more.

'No!' came a stiff reply. Tears welled up in Anya's eyes—angry tears—as she walked into her room and slammed the door shut.

Things had been hard for Anya in the past few months. Her family had shifted to a new city, and she had had to leave behind all her friends whom she'd known since childhood.

At her new school, Anya had managed to make two friends, Vivek and Nazia. But since these two had been friends with each other longer, there were times when Anya felt like an outsider in the equation. That is what had happened today too. Perhaps.

An hour later, Anya still had a lump in her throat. She noticed that her mother was busy in the kitchen. So, she quietly went out to the backyard. This was her favourite place in this house; whenever she wanted to be left alone, she sat here on some steps that overlooked a pond. Anya mechanically kept throwing stones into the water, while tears ran down her cheeks again.

'Someone has had a bad day, it seems,' a familiar voice interrupted Anya's thoughts.

'Oh? I didn't see you coming,' Anya said, as she looked up and saw Shakti standing near her. 'Well, you're right. I've had a very bad day.'

Anya loved talking to Shakti. Each time she'd been

in a foul mood, after shifting here, Shakti had helped her snap out of it. There was something very magnetic about the young girl. Anya often pondered: Was it her knowing smile? Her deep green eyes? Her manner of speech? Her mere presence? Or the fact that Shakti too didn't have any friends?

'Let me guess—it's something your new friends at school did.' Shakti prompted, as she sat down beside Anya.

'Is it so obvious?' Anya asked, confused.

'Well, you get most upset by the things they do. And today your eyes are swollen up like a frog's.'

A slight hint of a smile appeared on Anya's lips, only to fade away immediately.

'There was a pyjama party at Nazia's place day before. But they didn't even tell me about it. I overheard some others raving about it in class today. She had invited Shaina, but not me. You know, Nazia doesn't even like Shaina. Nobody likes Shaina. I am so upset. At least Vivek could have told me. Even he didn't. I feel so unwanted. I hate it!' Anya ranted and wept uncontrollably.

Shakti put her hand around Anya. 'I understand how much it hurts. But why don't you do something about it?'

'It's no use. When I confronted Nazia and Vivek, they said they thought I didn't like parties. Even if that's true, how can they not invite me!' Anya said angrily.

'By 'do something' I didn't mean confrontation,' Shakti rolled her eyes.

'Then?' Anya didn't understand.

'Anya, I think the time has come for me to share the most important episode of my life with you. Something that changed everything: my friends' lives and mine as well. But promise me, you will never tell anyone about it. Never!'

As Anya nodded and gazed into Shakti's eyes searchingly, Shakti began narrating ...

'Kunal, Yuvika and I were BFFs. We were always together. If one was unwell, the other two bunked classes and went to the sick one's house to spend time together. There were no secrets between us: the conversations I had with my cousins; at what time I went vegetable-shopping on Saturdays; how much water I drank in a day ... I told them everything. Similarly, they shared their lives with me. We led completely open lives.

But at our graduation party, something was different. Both of them exchanged glances and smiles every now and then without reason. It hadn't happened before; it was very different. In that moment, I realised that the equation had changed. I was still with them, and yet they were only with each other. As a hundred thoughts crowded my mind, a classmate walked up to us and congratulated Kunal and Yuvika.

'What's going on?' I finally asked them. 'Promise me you won't kill us,' Kunal joked.

'He proposed to me,' Yuvika interrupted, excitedly showing me her ring.

'You got engaged?' I muttered in shock.

'What? It had to happen someday,' Kunal shrugged.

I stared at them quietly. 'Shakti, stop pretending like you didn't know!' Yuvika slapped my arm jovially.

'I didn't! Why didn't you tell me?' I asked, trying hard to control my tears.

'Are you kidding me? What's there to tell? Everybody knows!' Kunal said matter-of-factly.

Everybody knows? The whole room swam in front of my eyes; I felt sick. The two people, who were my life, had hidden their relationship from me. They had said nothing about it. And the fool that I was, I had believed we were best friends forever. It dawned upon me that all along, I had been the third in that friendship. We had never really been equals. The more I thought about it, the dizzier I felt.

'Shakti, aren't you happy for us?' Yuvika looked sad.

'Congratulations!' I mumbled and hurried home.

I was so distraught that when I was crossing the street near my house, I didn't notice a speeding vehicle come my way.

The next couple of hours were the most difficult for my family and me. I could hear the doctor telling my parents I wouldn't make it. Do you see this scar around my neck going up to the back of my head? It's from that accident.

I'm sure Kunal and Yuvika wanted me to understand, but the truth is that they never understood. My pain didn't go, nor did my loneliness. That is when I decided what I must do next: I took them for an overnight stay to my ancestral haveli.

The haveli had been locked for years. But since it was our ancestral property, the keys were with my family. I'd visited it only once before, when I was a toddler. We never went back. Everyone believed the haveli was haunted ...'

A chill ran down Anya's spine. 'What happened at the haveli?' Anya asked hesitantly, engulfed by a sense of premonition.

Shakti stared at the still waters of the pond, smiled, and continued ...

'The rays of the full moon fell right into the Royal Blue Room of the haveli, where we sat and chatted for a long time. After a while, Yuvika was thirsty. Strangely, there was no water in the room, although we remembered we'd carried enough with us. The only other option was to go down to the backyard: dad had had a handpump installed there. I agreed to accompany her—I couldn't have left her alone.

But weird things started happening. As the two of us walked down the winding stairs, Yuvika kept turning back.

'Someone's following us' she said, frightened. I told her she was imagining things, and there really was no one.

We hurried through the dimly lit corridors, because she shut her ears and kept saying, 'The pillars are whispering my name, Shakti.' But I couldn't hear a thing.

On reaching the handpump, I asked Yuvika to stay calm, while I rapidly filled water in the bottles.

'Faster, Shakti, faster. Someone's watching us. Faster!' she kept repeating. Suddenly, she screamed. But before I could do anything, she was gone.'

'Where?' Anya asked timidly. 'Vanisshhed ... into thin air,' Shakti revealed in a hushed voice. The green of her eyes seemed deeper now. Instead of shock, Anya could oddly sense glee in her manner. Shakti continued to recount ...

'I looked around for Yuvika; called out her name a million times. Silence. She had disappeared right in my presence. I ran up to tell Kunal about it, but met him midway on the winding steps: he had heard Yuvika scream, and was coming downstairs to investigate. He went pale, as I told him what had just happened.

'Impossible!' he murmured. 'Is this a prank, Shakti? Because if it is, I am not liking it!' he shook me by my shoulders angrily.

'How can I make her disappear, Kunal?' I tried to reason. 'Let's look for her,' he said, regaining his composure.

We walked down the same corridor. And would you believe it, Kunal too said the pillars were whispering his name. As we entered the backyard, something more bizarre had happened: the handpump was missing, and there was just sand everywhere.

'Where's the water pump?' Kunal looked at me accusingly.

'I have no idea. It was right here,' I told him, looking as dumbfounded as him.

'Something eerie is going on, Shakti,' he said, as we went back into the haveli.

'You hear that?' Kunal said suddenly, when we were passing through the pillared corridor. 'It's Yuvika. She's calling for help.' Again, I couldn't hear anything at all.

'I understand you are troubled by her disappearance, Kunal, but don't let that mess with your mind,' I tried to calm his nerves.

But he didn't listen to me. 'Some dark force is at work here. Yuvika ... Yuvika ...,' he called out, running deeper and deeper into the haveli in search of that voice—Yuvika's voice.

Kunal was too fast; I couldn't keep pace with him. Soon, his voice faded into the distance, until I heard it no more. I had heard stories of the haveli having been built like a maze. And they used to say that almost no one found their way back out of it.

In the matter of an hour, I had lost both my friends. I felt deep sorrow. But that was momentary, for a certain sense of peace took over. We should have stayed together—the three of us. But they chose to leave me out, didn't they?'

Abruptly ending her chilling tale, Shakti turned to Anya: 'Now you know why I am here, talking to you. I have been helping distressed girls like you—who have horrible, insensitive friends—for ages.

You should avenge your pain, your humiliation, your loneliness ... After all, you're as alone as me. Take Vivek and Nazia to my haveli. It will give you peace.'

Anya felt as though Shakti had changed; she seemed different, almost abnormally non-human. Mustering up courage, Anya asked her slowly, 'H ... how come nothing happened to y ... you at the haveli?'

Shakti's lips spread into a wide, creepy smile. Cocking her head slightly, she looked at a petrified Anya and whispered forebodingly, 'Why do you think?'

Anya felt powerlessly drawn towards Shakti's green, hypnotic eyes.

A hand reached out from behind and touched Anya on her shoulder lightly. She jumped up, screeching in fright.

'It's okay, it's me,' her mother comforted her.

'Mom!' Anya hugged her mother tightly, shaking with fright. 'It's nothing, Anya. I'm sorry I scared you,' her mother kissed her sweaty forehead. 'I've told you so many times sitting out alone in this cold isn't good for you. You'll catch a chill and it's not even safe,' her mother went on, as both of them began strolling back towards their house.

Alone? Didn't mom see Shakti? Anya wondered. And in a flash, her eyes widened with disbelief: But how could it be? Shakti seemed so real. Maybe Anya was hallucinating.

Slowly, she turned behind to check if Shakti was still there. She was! The confusion cleared and Anya started seeing the truth: Shakti's accident! Which means that the Shakti who took Kunal and Yuvika to the haveli was not alive ...!

As the retreating figure of Shakti continued to stare at her unblinkingly, fear stayed in Anya's eyes.

That night Anya's father asked her mother, 'You look worried. What's the matter?'

'This whole shifting business, it is affecting Anya badly,' she said. 'Come on, not again. You are getting paranoid now,' he argued. 'Today, I saw Anya talking to someone near the pond ...'

'Isn't that good? She's making new friends,' he interrupted her. 'There was no one there! And when I went over to her, she freaked out,' her mother said nervously.

Anya's father thought for a second before mumbling, 'Well, she must have been talking to ... herself, because she is lonely. She's a child. Children usually do that.'

'I think it is something else ...' Anya's mother's voice quivered. 'Something else? What do you mean?'

'You remember the maid told us about the ghost of a girl who had no friends haunting this place ...'

'Stop right there! You're a doctor, for heaven's sake! Keep your sanity ... I'll talk to Anya tomorrow. Trust me, everything will be fine,' he hugged his wife comfortingly.

'I hope so. I really hope so,' she repeated, tears spilling out of her unsure eyes.

The next day Anya didn't go to school. She didn't speak to anyone at home. However, unknown to her parents, she made two phone calls—one, to Vivek, and the other, to Nazia.

By evening, Anya's house was in a state of utter chaos. Her parents were running helter-skelter, frantically calling out her name and looking for her everywhere. Anya was missing.

'This is such a crazy plan, Anya. I love it. Running away from school and home to spend a night in a so-called "haunted house",' Vivek chuckled, as he excitedly pushed open the door of the Royal Blue Room of a haveli.

'Wow! It's a gorgeous mansion,' Nazia remarked, marvelling at the ornate room.

'So, what's the plan? Anya? Hey, Anya?' Vivek called out to Anya from behind, who stood staring at a portrait on the wall.

'We're going to have fun, friends!' Anya whispered, as she turned to face them.

Vivek and Nazia grew pale, and stood immobilised on seeing her: A sharp cut had suddenly appeared near Anya's neck and it travelled to the back of her head; Anya's eyes had changed colour to a deep green; her smile, uncanny; her skin, pale; and her demeanour, disturbing ... as though she were possessed!

CLASS SEVEN LEARNS A LESSON

Arundhati Venkatesh

Alaap and Paavni were singing one of their silly jugalbandis. Gaurav added to the cacophony, with his 'desk drums'. 'Stop banging the desk!' Roshni pushed her glasses up on her nose and tried to focus on the Rubik's cube. 'How do I get this orange square to the other side? All I need is two minutes of silence,' she muttered.

Gaurav grinned and banged even harder.

Roshni put her hands over her ears, scowling at him. Alaap belted out,

'Yippee! We are free!
No teacher, you see.
Poor Princey Baggy
Has to let us be-e-e!'

Paavni chimed in,

'C'mon, sing with me!'

'May I have some silence please, if you don't mind? Just two minutes will do.' Roshni's voice dripped with sarcasm. 'No hurry ... whenever you're done singing your Grammy-winning song.'

'Oh, go climb a tree,' Paavni sang with a flourish.

Roshni pressed her hands more tightly over her ears. It was no use. She put the Rubik's cube away.

'Noisier than a fish market,' Mrs Chatterjee would have said. In just a fortnight, they had driven away all their teachers. Mrs Chatterjee had been the first.

On the first day of Class Seven, Mrs Chatterjee had begun her recital with great gusto, 'Where the mind is without fear and the head is held high ...'

Gaurav chose that very moment to let Choochoo out of his trouser-pocket. Yes, that pest Gaurav had a pet mouse.

Mrs Chatterjee forgot all about being fearless. She clambered onto the table and began screeching like a fire alarm. Choochoo thought it was a game and squeaked even louder.

'What is it?' Kashibai had come running, 'I could hear the screams in the toilet.'

Kashibai's eyes grew as big as brinjals when she saw Mrs Chatterjee crouched atop the table.

'Meydum?' Kashibai looked at her questioningly. Mrs Chatterjee whimpered, pointing at the mouse.

Kashibai burst into giggles. 'Meydum, meydum,' she kept sighing as she ran after the excited mouse, broom in hand.

After an hour of playing tag, Kashibai managed to trap Choochoo in the dustbin.

'Oh no! My Choocho-o-o-o-o,' Gaurav had wailed. 'She'll drown him in a bucket of water.'

'If you don't stop crying, we'll drown in your tears,' Roshni snapped.

Harpreet looked smug. 'I'll swim.'

'I didn't mean it literally. Oh, forget it.'

Kashibai hurried out of the classroom, dustbin in hand. Mrs Chatterjee scurried after her.

That was the last they saw of Mrs Chatterjee.

Mrs Pinto was their next target. This time, Yukti had custom- created the weapons of mass destruction. They looked like crossbows, but were built entirely of sticks and rubber bands. 'Attack!' Yukti yelled, while Mrs Pinto painstakingly derived a trigonometry theorem on the board.

It was a synchronised operation. Gaurav, Paavni, Alaap, Harpreet, Rizwan and Yukti took position and aimed at Mrs Pinto. Missiles rained on her from all directions.

After the second such drone strike, Mrs Pinto had stormed out of the classroom, never to return.

'Retired hurt,' Gaurav had ticked off her name in the register. One after the other, Class Seven had got rid of all the teachers.

All except Mr Shanmugam. He had given them a tough time. He was as thick-skinned as a buffalo. He cheerfully withstood all their onslaughts in the classroom. Until Rizwan masterminded the winning plan.

Mr Shanmugam had been reading aloud from Ruskin Bond's *A Face in the Dark*, when Rizwan had a brainwave. He whispered the plan into Paavni's ear. For the next fifteen minutes, Paavni couldn't stop snorting into her handkerchief. Everyone knew she was trying hard not to laugh, but Mr Shanmugam thought it was a fit of wheezing and sent for Nurse Cheriyamma.

'Nothing wrong with her ... physically,' the nurse eyed Paavni suspiciously. 'We'll keep her under observation anyway,' she'd declared. Paavni spent the next hour in the dispensary. Meanwhile, Rizwan scribbled his idea on a piece of paper and passed it around.

It was a stroke of genius.

That night, Mr Shanmugam heard strange sounds outside his door, like a kitten scratching. He threw open the window to check. What he saw next made him let out a blood-curdling scream.

The ghostly white apparition was unlike anything he had seen before. Its many heads bobbed up and down in the moonlight. Its torso swayed like bamboo in the gentle breeze. The ghost let out a low moan. Then a deep grunt.

A shrill call. A howl. A raspy growl. A high-pitched shriek. The creature had six distinct voices. Mr Shanmugam stood transfixed.

The next morning, Baggy—that's what everyone called the Princey, Mrs Bagalkot—launched a search operation for Mr Shanmugam.

There was fear written all over the teachers' faces. They spoke in hushed tones. 'It's a mystery.' 'There's no trace of him.'

Nurse Cheriyamma's voice rang out, 'Which coconut in this school had the guts to mess with me?'

All the classes poured into the passage, curious to see what the coconut had done, and eager to see what fate the coconut would meet with.

Nurse Cheriyamma stomped down the corridor, screaming, 'Who dared poke holes in my sparkling white bedsheet?'

Paavni began snorting into her handkerchief again. Back she went to the dispensary.

'He's disappeared. Just like that.' The teachers were still thinking of Mr Shanmugam. They stood around, wringing their hands.

'I thought I saw someone like him running towards the railway station,' Kashibai wiped her hands in the folds of her sari. 'I can't say for sure; it was dark and I was squatting far away in the fields.'

No one paid any attention to her.

The news spread fast. Mr Shanmugam had vanished without a trace, and a supernatural force was to blame. The police were too terrified to investigate. None of the teachers had the guts to enter the classroom after that. Class Seven is jinxed, they said. Baggy was at her wit's end. She put out an advertisement in the newspaper.

WANTED: A HIGH SCHOOL TEACHER.
QUALIFICATIONS: SHOULD BE UNFLAPPABLE.
EASILY FLUSTERED CANDIDATES NEED NOT APPLY.

There were no applicants.

Clearly, there were no fearless adults in all of Chikwad district.

The students of Class Seven were unruffled. They settled into a comfortable routine. Roshni tried to improve her timing at the Rubik's cube. Rizwan and Harpreet played Monopoly. Yukti made a manual for her latest invention. Gaurav, Alaap and Paavni made a nuisance of themselves.

All that was about to change.

'Did you hear that?' Rizwan nudged Roshni.

'I can't hear anything above this din,' Roshni grumbled. 'All I want is some quiet. Is that too much to ask for?'

'Shhhhh!'

Tap, tap, tap ... the sound echoed in the corridor. 'Long John Silver,' Rizwan whispered.

'What?' Harpreet asked.

'The pirate. That sounds like his crutch.'

Harpreet sat with her eyes glued to the door, waiting for the dreaded pirate to hobble in on his crutch.

A tall, scrawny man in a black suit walked in with an ornate walking stick in one hand and something like a laptop bag in the other.

'My grandfather has one like that.' Yukti pointed to the bag. 'It's called a briefcase. I use it to store my manuals.'

No adult had entered the room in weeks. Except Kashibai. The old lady cleaned the place every day. Who

was this man who had dared to take on the dreaded spirit that lurked in Class Seven?

His cheeks were sunken, his nose sharp, like a crow's beak. He was all bones from head to toe, as if he hadn't eaten in a long time. He stared at them with piercing eyes.

'He must be a lawyer,' Harpreet gasped. 'Mr Shanmugam must have filed a case against us for trespassing on his property. Remember that board I stubbed my toe against that night? It said, 'TRESPASSERS WILL BE PROSECUTED.'

'I hear there's a ghost that haunts this room.' The skinny man had a booming voice.

'Those are just rumours,' Yukti spoke up. 'There's no such thing.' The tall man drew a sharp breath. 'You don't believe in ghosts, young lady?'

'No,' Yukti sniggered.

'Haven't met the undead yet, eh?' he chuckled.

'The undead?' Yukti rolled her eyes.

'Perhaps you'll change your mind after you hear me out,' he leered. 'I realise I haven't introduced myself. I'm Mr Ullagaddi.'

'He speaks like a classic!' Roshni mumbled.

'Who's sick?' Paavni turned around.

'Nobody,' Roshni answered impatiently. 'I said 'classic'. Like the works of Shakespeare, Charles Dickens ...'

'I was just having fun rhyming. Ha ha!'

Roshni stuck her tongue out at Paavni. She turned her attention to what Mr Ullagaddi was saying.

'What is it but vanity to imagine that there is no world but this?' He was flailing his arms. 'That there are no other people inhabiting the universe but humans like you?'

Roshni twisted the Rubik's cube under the desk.

'Do you have courage to face reality, that there are different worlds, different kinds of people?' He had a sudden bout of coughing. 'Akhuh akhuh ...' He did seem very ill.

He continued when the coughing had subsided, 'The undead are a people too, with their own laws, government ...' He paused again.

Harpreet sprang up with her water bottle. Mr Ullagaddi waved her away.

'... and the Society for the Prevention of Cruelty to Humans. The last time a new government was elected, a legislation was passed banning the consumption of human flesh.'

Society for the Prevention of Cruelty to *Humans*? Roshni sneered.

'There was widespread dissent, but the government did not relent. For centuries and millennia, the undead has consumed human meat, but that was no longer permitted. Slowly, things began to change. While many adapted to the new ways, some suffered. A few rebelled. Every now and then, there would be news of someone instigating a revolt. One such rebel was Albert.'

The wind whooshed, bringing down thatched roofs and branches. Rain lashed against the windows. Roshni stared at the colours on the Rubik's cube, mesmerised.

Rizwan closed the windows on Mr Ullagaddi's instructions. The storm raged on outside, but all was quiet in the classroom. 'Albert had an insatiable appetite. The ban had a devastating effect on him. He grew weaker and weaker. Albert had to eat humans, he just had to. Where do you think he went to feed?'

Mr Ullagaddi waited. There was no response, not a sound.

'He went to morgues,' Mr Ullagaddi went on. 'He fed on decomposed human flesh. The secret service found out his modus operandi and reported him to the government. Security was beefed up at entry points to all morgues.'

'What did Albert do?' Alaap asked.

'It's a long story. Why don't you make yourselves comfortable? Your braces must hurt. Take them off. Put them away. Take off your shoes too.'

There was a flurry of activity.

'Cheeee!' Paavni made a face. Everyone held their noses.

Someone's socks were stinking!

'Must be Gaurav's,' Roshni muttered.

Mr Ullagaddi took a deep breath and smiled. He was relishing the smell!

There was no telling what smells people liked. Roshni's little cousin loved to dig his nose into her armpits!

'Time stands still when you're listening to a good story,' he said when he had stopped sniffing. 'Who needs watches? In they go!'

'You! Your glasses will come in the way. Take them off.' Roshni looked up to see Mr Ullagaddi staring down at her.

'Take them off? Why?' Roshni kept her glasses on.

'Questions, questions!' Mr Ullagaddi grew impatient. 'Just do as I say. All will be clear by the end of the day.'

'But I won't be able to see without them.'

'Don't you dare argue with me!'

Something in his tone made Roshni take off her glasses.

'So what did Albert do?' Alaap butted in. 'How did he survive if he couldn't get into a morgue?'

'Not one to give up easily, he switched to hospitals, where there was an abundance of rotting flesh. He was a master of disguise, but the secret service caught up with him. Albert was sentenced to eternal imprisonment and carted off to the dungeons. But he gave them the slip.'

'Where did he go? Where is he now?'

'Ah, the chief of the secret service would give her left arm to know,' he smirked.

'Ewww. The undead cut off their arms?' Harpreet grimaced. 'It's just an expression, silly,' Paavni shushed her.

'What does he look like?' Alaap asked.

'Does it matter what he looks like? You humans! You are too preoccupied with physical appearance.'

Roshni gasped. She felt an icy chill descend on her. She looked around desperately, but everything was blurred. She could see Gaurav if she squinted hard. She opened her mouth, but no words came out. 'How will we identify Albert if we ever encounter him?' Alaap continued. He didn't seem to realise anything was amiss. 'Does he have horns? Or fangs?'

'No horns. And Albert's fangs were damaged permanently by braces, watches, whatnot. He had to have them extracted and replaced with silver caps. That's such a comedown for the undead.'

Roshni worked the Rubik's cube furiously. The little squares began to fall into place.

'Akhuh! Akhuh!' Another coughing bout.

Roshni shuddered. Her hands shook. The Rubik's cube fell to the floor. She went down on her knees, fumbling for the cube under the desk. If only she had her glasses on! She was still groping in the dark, when the screaming started.

Roshni cowered in terror. The shrieking and howling went on for what seemed like eternity. Roshni recognised the voices. Paavni's shrill voice. Gaurav's threatened growl. Alaap's raspy voice. One by one, the voices died out. The silence was deafening. Roshni wished she could hear something, anything—Alaap and Paavni singing, even Gaurav drumming. Would she never hear any of them again? Ever? Roshni felt tears streaming down her cheeks. She crouched under the desk, trembling.

Tap, tap, tap ...

The tapping grew louder. And louder.

And LOUDER.

Something glinted in the distance. It was coming towards Roshni. It stopped right under her nose. Roshni's eyes travelled upwards from the brass carving at the bottom of the walking stick. Mr Ullagaddi's face appeared, barely inches away from the tip of her nose. He broke into a grin, revealing four silver caps. Roshni stifled a scream.

His hands rose to his face, very slowly. He pulled something off and tossed it aside. A mask!

The skin beneath was shrivelled, the face ravaged with ghastly tears, the lower lip puffed up like a balloon. The upper lip was badly mauled and decaying. There were dried purple crusts where his ears and nose should have been. Pus oozed out of his eyeballs. Worms crawled out of the pores on his skin. Maggot-infested sores covered his neck.

He held out a disfigured, worm-eaten hand. 'I am Ullagaddi.

Roshni heard herself shriek. A putrid odour permeated the room. There was a deep, guttural moan.

And then deathly silence.

C&R

Shabnam Minwalla

Sophia and Tariq were part of a large, noisy family. There were plenty of cousins with foreign accents and grand-aunts with loud cackles. They gathered in Mumbai every couple of years to attend weddings, eat mangoes and shop. And on one evening, all the cousins would make their excited way to their grandparents' apartment in Colaba. They would climb the steep, creaky staircase, eat an enormous dinner and huddle in the vast hall full of antique chairs and shadowy corners and wait for Salim Uncle to start.

As uncles go, Salim was young. He was a student in an American university and a great teller of tales. Especially ghost stories. His sessions were conducted after dark, with the lights switched off, the curtains drawn, the doors shut and props in place—a clacking rosary, a brazier of glowing coals, a mirror. Sophia could never decide whether she enjoyed these evenings or abhorred them. But for Tariq they were the highlight of the year.

Salim Uncle usually started out with pleasantly scary stories. The tale of the bleeding house near New York. Then the one about the spectral dog with a flaming head that visited an old Bombay bungalow.

By this point the littler cousins were whimpering and had to be sent to bed. After which, Salim Uncle would shut the doors and draw the curtains even tighter and assume a grim expression. 'C and R musn't hear us,' he would whisper. And an uneasy shiver would run through the people in the room.

Sophia was never sure how serious Salim Uncle was—but she felt compelled to check the windows every few minutes, terrified that two hideous, gloating faces would be pressed against the glass.

Chamanai and Ratanai were the most notorious and eerie ghosts in the Bohra Muslim community. The two women had lived a long time ago. Their graves sat in a sinister corner of a cemetery in Surat. And even the most rational adults avoided uttering their names. 'If you say their names aloud, they will come,' Salim Uncle would warn them. 'Avoid talking about them. If you must talk about them, refer to them as C and R. Never say their full names, especially at dusk. And never, never stand in a corner and say their names. Because when you turn around, they will be waiting just behind you AND ...'

At this point, Sophia would block her ears and squeeze her eyes shut.

These, of course, were only the statutory warnings. Then came the story.

Chamanai and Ratanai were mother and daughter and lived in Surat hundreds of years ago. Chamanai always wore black and Ratanai always wore red. Ratanai was married to a very holy man and soon got bored of his preaching and do-gooding and poisoned him. At the moment of his death, every single mirror in the house cracked.

After Chamanai and Ratanai died, the two evil spirits—one black and one red—wandered the twisty, narrow lanes of Bohra Mohalla in Surat. They were experts in the art of disguise and could pretend to be a kind aunty or a charming stranger. They would befriend their victim, wangle an invitation to their house and finally reveal their true nature.

Then the two ghosts would glide inexorably towards their cowering victim, their faces leering, their eyes glittering with evil. And all it took was a single look at their malevolent smiles for the hapless victim to collapse.

Eventually the two spirits were trapped in bottles by a brave fellow named Mirbhai Moosa who used a combination of trickery and prayers to nab them. He then buried the bottles in a deserted stretch of countryside. And everybody breathed a sigh of relief.

Years later, a railway track was being laid between Surat and Bombay. Workers were digging the ground when they unwittingly smashed two bottles. To their amazement, black and red smoke swirled out and floated away.

At that exact moment, mirrors all across Surat cracked. Chamanai and Ratanai were back.

'Then?' Sophia would ask hopefully.

'Then, nothing,' Salim Uncle would reply. 'They're still out there somewhere. Waiting to be summoned. If you see pieces of red and black cloth fly past, be very careful. If a strange woman in red or black talks to you, be very careful.'

'But what can we do?' one of the cousins would ask tremulously.

'Check her feet,' Salim Uncle would reply immediately. 'C and R have feet that point backwards. And they don't walk. They glide about one inch above the ground. Those are the only things that they cannot disguise.'

'And what if ... what if the stranger's feet point backwards ... what then?' Sophia once asked.

'Then be careful not to look at her directly in the face. Be careful never to invite her to your house. And keep your wits about you. If you see through C and R's disguise and refuse them entry, they can never harm you again.'

Sophia was so terrified of Chamanai and Ratanai that she did actually peep at the feet of strange women for many years. Then she became a teenager and more interested in fashion and pop songs than ghosts. She coloured her hair, wore tight t-shirts and listened to the Top 40s. And she forgot to be afraid.

After school, Sophia joined St Xavier's College in Mumbai. She loved her new subjects, especially Psychology and History. So when the Psychology teacher gave the class its first assignment, she was determined to do it well.

'It's about the power of stories,' she explained to her family at dinnertime. 'About how certain stories capture the imagination of a certain group or community. We have to find one story, and describe its hold on a group of people.'

'How interesting!' her mother remarked, passing around the rice. 'Have you thought of anything?'

'I don't know,' Sophia replied, tapping the table with a spoon. 'Some fable, I guess.'

'Why not C and R?' Tariq asked suddenly.

'C and R?' Sophia repeated.

'Chamanai and Ratanai, your favourite spooks,' he said, serving himself chicken.

'Don't say their names,' his mother snapped automatically. 'And why that story, of all the stories in the world. Some things are better left alone.'

Tariq laughed. 'There you are. All of you are scared witless of those two characters. Nobody says their names. Nobody goes near their graves. What better proof do you need about the power of stories?'

Sophia nodded enthusiastically. It was a great idea.

The next morning, Sophia sat at her computer and conducted a Google search for Chamanai and Ratanai. To her astonishment, she didn't get a single hit. Nothing at all.

'Your search—chamanai ratanai—did not match any document,' the screen informed her. 'Did you mean chamana urbana or chandni raatein?'

Sophia meant neither. So she tried Chamanbai and Ratanbai instead. This time she got a few matches. But the various Chamanbais and Ratanbais were names on government lists and court documents. There wasn't the slightest indication that they were anything other than ordinary mortals.

'It's bizarre,' Sophia told Tariq that evening. 'You can find every possible thing on the internet. But nothing at all about these most famous ghosts!'

'Maybe everybody's too scared to write about them,' Tariq shrugged. 'Anyway, you can ask Salim Uncle. Or Ruby the Rajdhani Express. Or Aunty Fatima.'

Sophia called a few cousins and aunts, all of whom seemed startled by her questions. They were all terrified of Chamanai and Ratanai, but were vague about the details. It was as if these two shadowy figures got their power from the silence and uncertainty that shrouded them.

Sophia made copious notes for her assignment. Salim Uncle—now an overworked professor in California—sent a terse email, filling in a few blanks. So the next day Sophia headed for the college library, planning to write her first draft.

The library—a high-ceilinged room awash with golden light—was full of students. Sophia shyly headed to one of the long polished tables and squeezed herself into a corner, next to two girls who were referring to enormous books on Microbiology. The girls ungraciously shifted their teetering stack and made space for the newcomer.

Sophia pulled out her pad and began writing the story of Chamanai and Ratanai. As she scribbled, long forgotten anecdotes floated back into her mind. She remembered her grandmother's sister who stoutly maintained that she had seen a red figure at the bottom of the staircase, just minutes before she tumbled down and broke her hip. Then she remembered the warnings about black and red fabric and Salim Uncle's words, 'Never, never say their name when you are standing in a corner. It is a clear invitation and they will come.'

After writing for half an hour, Sophia stopped to stretch and look idly around the library. Then she read her draft to herself in a low mumble. A habit that always bugged Tariq—and seemed to displease her Microbiology-loving neighbours as well.

Sophia was making a few corrections when a dark shadow passed over her yellow pad. She looked up sharply. And then she saw it.

A red handkerchief.

It had appeared on the table behind the Microbiology books.

Just an ordinary red hanky.

Except that as Sophia stared, she felt a jolt like an electric shock. A sudden, sickening realisation that made her fingers numb and her head spin. And as she sat, clinging onto her pen and sanity she knew—without knowing how—that they were here.

Chamanai and Ratanai were here.

Terror gripped Sophia so hard that she could barely breathe. She had been stupid and foolhardy. She had broken all the rules. She had sat in a corner and uttered names that were better forgotten. And someone ... something ... had heard.

'Stop it. It's just a handkerchief. It's just a stupid ghost story,' Sophia tried to calm herself. But it was futile. She could feel the prickle of evil. She could identify the whiff of malevolence in that bright, busy room.

Desperately, Sophia turned to the Microbiology students and pointed to the red hanky with a shaking finger and asked, 'Is that yours?'

The two girls gave her a strange look and merely shrugged. The hanky fluttered faintly in the breeze—and suddenly Sophia was galvanised into action. She grabbed her notes and file and pens, squashed them into her backpack, and rushed out of the library.

She charged out of the college, down the road and only stopped when she reached her bus stop. She was still panting when a 132-numbered double decker bus arrived and she climbed to the upper deck, sank into a vacant seat and squeezed her eyes shut. A few minutes later, feeling calmer, she opened her eyes and looked around.

Everything was normal. Young boys with mountainous school bags. A dispirited looking carpenter. A group of villagers babbling excitedly. Then suddenly Sophia's gaze fell on the empty seat next to her. And she let out a piercing shriek.

On the seat—just two inches away from her—was a flimsy, black chiffon dupatta.

The other passengers were most concerned. But Sophia pushed past them and jumped out of the bus at a traffic signal. She stumbled all the way home and was flushed and feverish when she arrived. Her mother fed her chicken soup and Crocin and firmly put her to bed.

By the next day, it was clear that Sophia had a viral infection. Her temperature soared and she lay on her pink bedspread with cold compresses on her forehead. She felt she was blundering through a grey, unpleasant dream.

Then one night she woke up with a start. Even before she looked at the window she knew, with complete clarity, what she was going to see. But still she gasped when she saw the twisted faces—indistinct in the inky night—before they disintegrated into the darkness.

Gradually the fever receded. But Sophia remained pale and miserable. She ate little, slept badly and was reluctant to leave the house. The sense of foreboding grew and grew. As did the conviction that Chamanai and Ratanai were just around the corner.

Finally, Sophia confided in her mother. 'I know it sounds like I'm imagining things,' she said tearfully. 'But they are out there. Sometimes I hear laughter that nobody else seems to hear. And I feel somebody's watching me.'

Sophia's mother was panic-stricken. Either Sophia was imagining terrible things or she was the victim of dark forces. Both options were alarming. She sent Uncle Salim a frantic email, but he was no help at all. 'I've always treated C and R as characters in a story,' he wrote. 'But maybe you could approach a priest. And explain to Sophia that she mustn't give in to irrational fears and beliefs. I can't think of anything else to do. So sorry.'

Sophia's parents began discreetly hunting for a priest with expertise in ghosts. Meanwhile, they insisted that Sophia should lead a normal life. 'No more locking yourself in the bedroom,' her mother said firmly. 'You love Navratri. You must attend your college dandia tomorrow. Go with Maira and Trisha. You'll have fun.'

So on Saturday evening, Sophia was getting dressed in a purple and pink ghagra choli when the doorbell rang. It was dusk—that time of day when all bad things come out to play—and Sophia was uneasy. But her parents had popped out to buy a microwave oven and Tariq was in the bathroom. So she forced herself to answer the door.

She looked through the peephole and saw a woman and a little girl in the late evening gloom. They were dressed in mirrorwork ghagra cholis and looked like everybody else that she knew. So Sophia opened the door.

The woman was glamorous in her shimmering skirt and beautifully streaked hair. 'Hi,' she said gaily, 'I'm Geeta Sukhija's sister. We've gotten here a bit too early and Geeta's stuck in traffic. Can we wait at your place for a few minutes? Love your ghagra choli, by the way.'

Geeta Sukhija lived one floor down and was a friendly, helpful soul. So Sophia held the door open and smiled at the little girl.

The child grinned back and licked her lips. Her tongue was a shocking red.

Sophia had opened her mouth to say 'come in'. But the words shrivelled up on her lips and, instead, she glanced at her visitors' feet. But they were completely covered by long and bulky ghagras.

Sophia felt giddy with indecision. She was afraid. But that was no reason to be rude to Geeta Aunty's sister. She had to get a grip on herself. Determined to do the polite thing, she started to wave them in. But all the time she could hear Salim Uncle's voice pounding in her head, 'Check their feet. Check their feet.'

Suddenly, Sophia knew what she must do. 'Please remove your shoes first,' she said in a loud voice.

The little girl glared with burning intensity. The woman hissed.

They both whirled around and vanished into the staircase.

Sophia shut the door, almost crying. Was she going mad? When would life return to normal? When would she stop seeing Chamanai and Ratanai in every stranger? Yes the two visitors had behaved oddly, but they could have been perfectly normal people!

Unsure of what she had done, Sophia headed to her dressing table to complete her make-up.

The lipstick was halfway to her lips when she saw it. The mirror had cracked from side to side.

THE CAT ON THE WINDOW

Sowmya Rajendran

Samina did not like the cat. It wasn't that she disliked cats in general. She didn't mind them. If you pressed her to tell you what exactly she thought of cats, she'd say that she preferred them to the average slobbery dog. But this cat ... it made her uneasy.

Maybe it was the face. Thin and pointed with large, yellow eyes. A small pink nose that reminded her of dried chewing gum. Its fur was grey, striped like that of a tiger. It belonged to the man upstairs, Mrs Gupta said.

Mrs Gupta knew the intimate secrets of all her neighbours (she had, for instance, been the first to know that Mr Ravikrishnan walked that way because of his piles) but even she did not know anything about the man who owned the cat. Not even his name! The nameplate on the door said Mr Chandrakumar but that was the name of the retired bank manager who owned the flat. He lived in America now with his son and Hispanic daughter-in-law, constantly amazed by the beautiful baby they had produced between them—its skin such a singular shade of caramel.

Mrs Gupta had tried to find out the mystery man's name by opening his mailbox but there was absolutely nothing inside it. She was convinced that he was either a drug dealer or a CIA agent. The man stepped out of the house rarely. And when he did, it was only to buy milk or the newspaper. 'I think he orders in all his meals,' Mrs Gupta confided to Samina. 'Imagine how unhealthy that is!' she said piously. Once, she'd tried to find out his name from the pizza delivery boy but the latter (a sweaty boy of nineteen with dark shadows beneath his eyes; a newly broken pimple on his chin) told her that the order was in the name of Mr Chandrakumar. Mrs Gupta was deflated. Where was the need to be so mysterious?

Samina was not too interested in the mystery man. By nature, she had no curiosity about things that were not immediately relevant to her life. But the cat now visited her every day and she could not stop thinking about it. It sat on the window shade outside her kitchen, looking in through the glass, watching her cook, following her movements as she stirred the kadai, went to the shelf to get the masala dabba, opened the fridge to get the milk out. At first, she ignored it. And then, when it started to make her feel uncomfortable, she tried to shoo it away. But the cat did not respond to her attempts. She considered opening the window and drenching it with a mug of water but she was afraid that it would scratch her. Or worse, climb into the house.

It was there in the morning when she came to make tea and it was there at night when she went to bed. Did it sleep there? Did it never eat? Samina assumed that whenever she stepped out of the kitchen after her work was done, the cat would go, too. It looked like a well-groomed animal although it was on the skinny side.

Rohit thought she was crazy to be so afraid of it. 'Even Arpita is not scared!' he said, when she told him one morning that the cat made her uneasy. Knotting his tie with expert hands, his familiar perfume filling the room, Rohit laughed at her fears indulgently. Arpita had, in fact, wanted to adopt the cat. For a moment, Samina wondered if she was losing her mind. She watched Rohit brush his hair in the mirror, staring at a spot in the white wall reflected on it till she thought she saw the shadow of the cat appear before her tired eyes.

And so, the cat stayed. It was around the same time that Arpita began to fall sick. She came down with a bad cold at first which later developed into a fever. When Samina took her to the doctor, he wrote down a blood test, suspecting that she was anaemic. The results confirmed this and Samina felt immensely guilty, thinking that she was responsible for her daughter's poor health.

'You look so pale,' she said, when they were on their way back home from the clinic. The roar of the autorickshaw filled her ears and made her head hurt.

'I'm fine,' said Arpita in a tight voice. Samina sighed. She knew teenagers were difficult and that her daughter was no different from millions of other adolescents. But still, it pained her sometimes to run into the cold walls within which Arpita chose to hide herself.

'It's all this dieting you are doing,' said Samina, unwilling to give up so easily. 'I told you it can't be healthy.'

'Don't bug me,' said Arpita, refusing to be dragged into an argument.

Mother and daughter sat in silence for the rest of the ride and by the time they were back home, Samina could barely hold her head upright. The headache threatened to split her skull open and she went to the kitchen to drink some water. There it was, the cat. It was staring at her with a smug expression in its eyes. As if it knew the pain she was in and was *happy* about it.

The next morning, Samina woke up early, determined to cook a healthy meal for her daughter. She knew it would lead to a war but she wasn't going to relent. Sometimes, a mother simply had to put her foot down. The cat watched her as she sliced the onions, its jaundiced eyes never leaving her.

'Ouch!' yelped Samina as the knife went through her skin. She sucked on her finger and examined the wound—it was only a light cut but there was blood pouring out of it. She caught a sudden movement in the corner of her eye and looked up. It was the cat, standing up now, peering at her with a strange

expression on its face. Samina realised with shock that it was hunger.

'Go away!' she yelled at it, putting a band-aid on the wound.

What was wrong with this animal?!

'Three rotis?' said Arpita disbelievingly, as she opened her box to see what her mother had packed for lunch.

'And mutton gravy,' said Samina brightly.

To her surprise, Arpita said nothing. She silently stuffed the box into her bag. Samina stared at her daughter's mutinous face. Her eyes looked so large, the thin skin on her face stretched across her skull tightly. With a shock, she realised that her daughter looked a lot like the cat. She shook her head to clear it of such ridiculous notions. The cat was ugly; her daughter was beautiful. Why was she thinking this way?

'Go and get ready,' Samina said through clenched teeth. 'Your school bus will be here soon.'

She went to the kitchen to toast the bread for breakfast. The cat was peering in now, scratching the glass and mewling, asking to be let inside. Samina suddenly felt furious. She wanted to pick up the cat and fling it from the window, not caring if it hurt her. She went close to the window and stared into its eyes. The cat paused its scratching and looked at her curiously, the black pupils in its yellow eyes alert and waiting. Samina noticed how plump it had grown, how much stronger. In panic, she imagined it crashing through the window, breaking the glass and landing on the floor, circling her in her own kitchen, as if she were a cornered mouse.

She ran from there then, right into the bedroom where Rohit was working on his laptop.

'Sam?' he said, noticing that she was sweating profusely. 'Everything okay?'

Samina sat down on the bed and nodded. She didn't want to tell him about the cat and have him laugh at her fears again. She didn't half believe herself. The idea that the cat was somehow responsible for Arpita's illness would seem so far-fetched to anyone with a rational mind. She wondered if she should go and talk to the owner about the cat. What if she knocked on his door till he opened it and she refused to leave till he gave her a solution?

Mustering her courage, Samina took the stairs and arrived at the mystery man's door, feeling a little breathless. She knocked softly at first and then harder when she heard no sounds of movement from inside. Was he out? She went on knocking desperately and suddenly turned when she heard footsteps. It was Mrs Gupta, come to see who was making such a ruckus. Samina was embarrassed. What was she going to tell her?

'Are you all right, dear?' asked Mrs Gupta, faking concern. Samina nodded and hastily began to walk away from the door, not wanting to answer any more questions. As she rushed downstairs, she saw the cat on the landing, crouching low, waiting.

Samina ran past it, trying hard not to look at its grotesque form—the fat body and the thin head, stuck to each other as if they were from two different animals.

When she was back home, Samina decided that that night, she would put an end to the cat's visits. She would hack it to death if necessary. She spent the entire day feeling jittery, avoiding the kitchen as much as possible. Rohit was going to be late coming home from work. He had a night call with his boss who was currently in the US and Samina knew that he wouldn't be back before 2 a.m. at the very least.

In the evening, when Arpita came back from school, her face sullen and drawn, Samina checked her lunch box to see if she'd eaten her lunch. Satisfied that it was wiped clean, Samina let Arpita be, without badgering her with her usual questions on homework and school lessons. She had too much on her mind in any case.

The moon was large and beautiful tonight. Samina crept out of the bedroom and opened the door to the kitchen. In the cold moonlight that bathed the black tiles of the walls, she saw her daughter standing by the window, staring outside. She was so still that Samina wondered for a moment if she was sleepwalking. And then, Arpita began to mewl softly. The cat whine filled Samina's heart with dread. She gasped in spite of herself. Hearing the noise, Arpita turned around, her plait flicking like the cat's tail. When she padded towards her mother, who lay collapsed against the door, the latter screamed at last.

A month earlier ...

'Fatty! Fatty!' God, it was that Mukund. Why couldn't he leave her alone? He called her names all the time and everyone else in class laughed like it was such a great joke. It was true that she was somewhat plump but was she really fat? Arpita pinched the skin on her arm to check and felt a wave of revulsion wash through her. She was going to become enormous if she kept eating like this. She felt like a blob of jelly as she walked up the stairs, sweating in her tight school uniform.

But if she didn't finish her lunch, Amma would be furious! It was then that she had a brainwave. Arpita dumped her lunch into a plastic cover and tied the top securely with a rubber-band. That night, after her parents were asleep, she opened the window in the kitchen and mewled, to attract the attention of the cat. 'Hey, kitty, hey kitty,' said Arpita. 'Look what I've brought for you!'

NOTHING IS WHAT IT SEEMS

Lubaina Bandukwala

There he is. Sitting on the ramparts. Alone. The sun is harsh and in the hazy light he looks like the vapour that rises from the bonfires of the night. Oddly formless.

Hoards of chattering tourists intermittently block my view as I stand in the shade of the pillared hall opposite. I feel strangely drawn to him, this boy. I want to reach out to him, talk to him. I brush past the tourists. They don't seem to have noticed the boy—it's as if only I can see him. Instead they stare in my direction, before they shrug their shoulders and walk away.

By the time I get past another group of day-trippers, he is gone, as always, just as I reach the ramparts. A deep sadness settles like a layer of desert dust over me. I am frustrated. I have missed him yet again.

He looks just like my boy, my nine-year-old, I think as I look down over the steep hillside falling far below the ramparts. I think of that day years ago when we came to see the magnificent fort. When he looked about him in wonder while I watched his happy face in equal wonder. And then. Then, one small step in the wrong direction, and the hillside took yet another life into its rock-strewn folds.

The loss brings me back to the fort. In every child I see I try to find my boy. Maybe he will appear out of the blue, knowing that I would come here everyday, long after the search parties had given up hope. Knowing that I would never give up hope that my boy will be with me once more.

I saw him for the first time a month ago. He appeared as if out of thin air on the ramparts of the fort just as the sun gasped its last breath and drowned in a sea of purples and

blues. Darkness rushed in, snapping at his heels, making him a mere shadow. But still he remained. Still.

I felt an odd sort of thrill. I wanted to talk to him, ask him why he was here long after all the visitors had gone. But I held back. Because, in this fort, nothing is as it seems. So I turned back, my pink sari flapping in the breeze and my footsteps softly clattering on the flagstone.

Yet another evening drew me to the ramparts and the boy. Will he be there again today? I think. Today I will go close. See him. Talk to him. My footsteps echo along the large empty courtyard. I will him to look at me. Slowly his head turns and he looks. Today, the rare shower of rain has washed the landscape, and darkness has fallen earlier than usual. Is it a trick of light? Or has his face lit up with that sweet smile?

'Coming, Ma!' he says! He's calling out to me! Oh happiness! But what is this? He turns and evaporates in the direction of the stone steps on the other side. Anger consumes me in great big gusts! Here! I am here! I cry soundlessly.

I must speak with him. I follow in a frenzy, propelled by grief, desperation. I try to hold him, and wrap my arms around him. He is slipping away like the mist. I am filled with rage, no, I will not let him go.

'Coming Ma!' the boy called out to his mother who lived in a small hut outside the fort, as he sped towards the steps. As he ran, he felt pinpricks of fear run down his spine. Over and over ma had told him not to sit on the ramparts after sunset. But he had scoffed her fears. However, lately he had had an odd feeling he was being watched. At first he could see nothing, just feel a gentle beckoning, inviting him to the pillared hall. And then tendrils of sadness reaching out to him as he ran back home in response to his mother's calls. Then, once or twice he caught a glimpse of a lady in a pink sari with a smiling face. And when he turned to leave the fort, he saw the face distort in rage and disappointment. Did he really see her? It was hard to make out, for in this fort nothing is what it seems.

Today particularly he felt a great sense of foreboding. An irrational fear gripped him. He quickened his steps looking around, but he was all alone. The tourists had all gone home. Before he reached the steps he felt a presence swooping upon him, closer and closer. He felt himself caught in an iron grip, yet he couldn't see anyone. Who was holding him? He struggled against this force he couldn't see. A dry sob rose up in his throat. It nudged him, engulfed him and pushed him inexorably towards the rampart, to its very edge.

The full moon rose and bathed the fort in blue. A high wind blew up the hillside and whistled past the thorny scrub. It wailed up the ramparts and caught in its crazed ebb and flow a blood-curdling sound.

Down on the hillside, a goatherd looked up at the darkening sky and hurriedly gathered the goats that had strayed farther than usual. As he hastened to reach his village, he stumbled upon the very marker he wanted to avoid. The stone that marked the spot where 20 years ago a widow fell to her death from the ramparts high above, while her terrified son looked helplessly on. He looked uneasily as the moon rose higher into the sky and when the long-drawn scream came to him on the wings of the wind, a chill ran down his spine. The widow's spirit had claimed yet another boy tonight.

CHARMINAR AND THE ROYAL GHOSTS

Vijay Marur

What happens to all the people who die? Once they become ghosts, do they carry on life with their families, with their wives and children? Do they continue to stay in their old houses, or do they move to another colony?

Are there like Daddy Ghosts and Mommy Ghosts ... children ghosts? And do children ghosts have rules?

Questions like these stumped Shyamala Ma'am. Especially because they were all raised by the rowdy bunch in Class 11.

Arrey baba, how am I supposed to know the answers to these questions? I'm just the History teacher, she murmured to herself. As she stepped into class, a huge black spider suspended on a thin string dropped down in front of her face. Shyamala Ma'am jumped backwards with a scream.

The whole class broke into an explosion of giggles and loud, derisive laughter.

Shyamala Ma'am bristled. This was too much. She decided to take revenge on this troublesome lot. Tease her, would they? She'd show them.

So she walked into class, waited for the noise to die down and then announced, 'Today we're going to discuss some ghost stories.'

Immediately, there was a hush in the class. This was a sudden twist. Ghost stories in class? Wow, how exciting!

'But there is no chapter on ghosts in our books Shyamala Ma'am,' objected one of the students.

'So what?', Shyamala Ma'am asked with a defiant expression on her face. 'Do you want to learn only what is in the textbooks? Are you not keen on learning something new?'

When the class nodded in agreement, she started.

'The first thing you have to understand and believe is that there are ghosts. There ARE ghosts. G H O S T S. Let no one tell you any different. And yes, there are many types of ghosts. Big and Small. Good and Bad. Safe and Dangerous. Male and Female. In fact, there are more ghosts in this world than real people.'

'How do you know that?' piped up Ramesh from the third row.

Irritating fellow.

'Simple,' she answered smugly. 'How many generations of your people have died? Your grandparents, their parents, their parents and so on, right? Let's say ten generations before you have all died and become ghosts ...'

'Yeah, yeah ... okay ... I get the picture,' admitted Ramesh as he sat down. But just as he sat down another doubt lit up his forehead.

'But Shyamala Ma'am ... where do all these ghosts stay?'

'In old houses of course,' ventured one student. And when he saw the other students nodding, he added, 'That's why they are called haunted.'

'Yes. Haunted houses house ghosts,' said Shyamala Ma'am, left with no choice but to agree with the majority.

And she loved the way the story was going. The kids were walking straight into her trap. Trouble her, would they? She'd show them. Make them so scared of ghosts and old houses that they would shiver to even walk past one of the many old buildings in the neighbourhood.

While the class was discussing different houses that they thought were haunted, one pair was not taking part. Young Qutub and Hyder. They were lost in exchanging glances, sneakily holding hands and generally looking lost in love.

That didn't surprise Shyamala Ma'am. She was quite used to it. This was a school romance that had been on since Class 10. Ever since the day Qutub had driven into school on a motorcycle. Preposterous, thought the school authorities. How wonderful, thought his peers.

Hyder of course began to adore him, even revere him that very moment. When exactly the near devotion turned to their version of love, no one could pin point, but it happened. It was inevitable, said everyone.

Anyway, they were significantly out of the ghost discussion. And Shyamala Ma'am did not like that one bit. In an attempt to include them in the class discussion, she asked Qutub to name a haunted house.

For a moment he looked irritated, as if upset that someone, even if she was the class teacher, had interrupted his daily regimen of love and romance. Then, in a sudden burst of energy, he said, 'Bhoot Bangla.'

And when he saw the derisive looks on his classmates' faces, he immediately corrected himself ... and spurted ... 'Charminar.'

The whole class reacted with different expressions of 'WHAT?'

Undeterred, he repeated, 'Charminar.'

Shyamala Ma'am couldn't take the insolence any more. 'Charminar!' She stretched in a high-pitched exclamation. 'What gives you the idea that Charminar is haunted?'

'Well it is one of the oldest buildings we know in Hyderabad. And you said ghosts haunt old buildings. So ... Charminar. Possibly the oldest ghosts in Hyderabad live there,' said young Qutub before he sat down again and began his 'romanchat' afresh.

'Shyamala Ma'am,' some of the other students asked. 'Can we go and check if there are actually ghosts in Charminar?' The question was innocent and she didn't know how to say no. So she said yes. And promised to arrange an excursion to Charminar.

'Can we go there at night,' someone asked. To that she had to say no because a night visit meant too many arrangements, permissions and what not.

So it was fixed. The whole class would be taken for an old city tour. They would be shown everything from Chaderghat Bridge to Purana Pul, from Purani Haveli to Chow Mohalla, from Shalibanda to Kabootar Khana. They would be taken for a walk on Laad Bazaar and then shown the Charminar. Lunch at Shadaab and dinner at Niagara, the iconic restaurants of the old city.

The plan was made and permissions got. Arrangements simply fell into place.

Never before had any excursion group seen the rest of the monuments in such a hurry. Never before had any group eaten so little. But it seemed that all the kids wanted to do, was to reach Charminar.

The bus stopped a few metres away from the four hundred and more-year-old monument and all the kids disembarked. They walked in a supervised straight line and entered the Charminar. They stood in an orderly fashion as the guide told them the story of Charminar. Qutub and Hyder laughed nervously as the story of the original Qutub Shah and Hyder Mahal was retold. Even the rest of the class sniggered a few nervous laughs.

Then the class was told to explore Charminar by themselves. 'Be careful children,' Shyamala Ma'am warned. The kids nodded and moved ahead hurriedly.

They climbed up the narrow stairs, ran their fingers on the many names hastily etched into the walls and kept looking out of the Charminar's many windows and skylights.

When they reached the point when they couldn't go any higher, the whole class looked around the monument at a world that was suddenly looking very small.

There was an autorickshaw that looked like an ant. And there was a miniature 'bandi' selling tiny bananas. The cars crawled around in an animated manner, almost like an insect parade. And there was a truck that was canvas-topped and looked like a cockroach.

The whole class had just started relaxing, taking selfies and photographs of each other, when suddenly

Qutub started shaking, gently at first, and then violently. The children next to him got worried but didn't know what to do. Hyder was obviously more concerned but she was as helpless. She looked for Shyamala Ma'am who was gazing lovingly at Laad Bazaar and screamed at her to help the shaken up Qutub.

With great difficulty Qutub was brought down to ground level. Cold water was found and sprinkled on the boy. Someone suggested putting a key into Qutub's mouth.

He seemed to be recovering, and relaxing. When suddenly he went quite rigid. His eyes rolled upwards and became glassy. He looked at Hyder and said in a strange voice, 'Come Hyder. Our people are waiting.'

He stood up as if possessed. He took Hyder's hand in his and walked out of Charminar before anyone could stop him.

The two walked down Laad Bazaar and a few hundred yards down, turned left. A few more regal steps, and they were at the famous Chowmahalla Palace. It was a mad procession. Qutub and Hyder in front. Walking as if in a trance. The rest of the class following blindly. Shyamala Ma'am was trying desperately to keep pace.

The entourage walked towards the gates of Chowmahalla Palace. They, however, were shut. But magically, almost on order, the gates opened. And the whole group entered the palace compound. Walking like zombies on the gravel path, they saw the fountains coming to life in the middle of the courtyard. Fairy lights came on. The trees looked like bejewelled courtiers swaying salaams to the King and Queen.

Qutub and Hyder walked straight to Khilwat, the Coronation Hall and on reaching the majestic throne, they sat down on it as if they had been doing it every day of their lives. The moment they sat down, the huge, recently refurbished chandelier lit up. The entire hall was bathed in a golden glow.

The rest of the class sat down on the marble floor. Even Shyamala Ma'am. They were tired after the brisk walk from Charminar to Chowmahalla. The palace guards, even the palace authorities stood around. Helpless. Clueless.

Suddenly, Qutub said, 'What are you all doing? Where are we?' Hyder suddenly realised that she was in the spotlight and she tried to walk away from the throne, but Qutub stopped her. She walked back to his side, albeit hesitantly.

'Let's go home, Shyamala Ma'am,' he said. 'It's getting late and our parents will get worried.'

Shyamala Ma'am gathered her wits and then gathered the children around. She called for the bus from Charminar. Qutub and Hyder boarded last, but not before Qutub stopped on the top step of the bus and looked lovingly at Chowmahalla.

The drive back to school was silent. Everyone was tired. No one wanted to talk about what they had seen. And quite honestly, some of them were a bit scared.

What had started as an excursion to see whether there were ghosts in Charminar had suddenly turned into something more mysterious and intriguing.

When Shyamala Ma'am got back to her house, she did not have the patience to cook herself a meal. So she just had a glass of milk and after some aimless television viewing, she went to sleep.

The next day at school everyone went about their normal routine without much of a fuss. Qutub and Hyder walked in as usual, holding hands, but they seemed not to remember what had happened the previous day. The rest of the class was uncharacteristically silent, and the whole day went by in a quiet, slow motion kind of way.

Shyamala Ma'am too went home that night in a kind of a daze. She knew something had happened, but didn't know how to describe it. If she spoke to her colleagues, she was afraid they would think her mad or unstable. So she just kept everything to herself.

She stepped into her house and made herself some simple dinner—some daal, a couple of rotis and one vegetable. She lay the table and went in to wash her hands and clean the kitchen. When she came back to the dining table she was surprised to see an extra bowl there. It had a portion of mirchi ka salan, a typical Hyderabadi dish.

Oh wow! thought Shyamala Ma'am when she spotted the extra dish. I must indeed be tired. I don't even remember cooking this dish. She had her dinner and the salan (curry) was really nice. Next day, she was back in school and greeted by a normal class. She taught her subject. And nodded with satisfaction when her students learnt to tell the difference between William Tell and William the Conqueror.

Back home for dinner that night, she was quite awake and quite sharp. So she knew that she had made only some plain rice and a mutton curry. So, imagine her surprise when she saw an extra bowl with a portion of chicken korma and some dahi ki chutney.

Shyamala Ma'am began to get worried. And that was not usual. Maybe I am too tired and my memory is playing tricks on me, she thought to herself. But she was not quite convinced. Let me wait one more evening, she thought as she put away the dishes and went to sleep.

The next day, she called a friend of hers over for dinner. And told her that the menu for the night was just a simple meal of rice, khatti daal, shammi kebabs and some kheer. At 7 pm, when the friend arrived she took her to the dining table and showed her the dishes she had made. Then the both of them settled down with a bottle of wine and talked about all that happened to each of them in the last couple of weeks when they hadn't met.

When Shyamala Ma'am started telling her Charminar story, the lights went off, plunging the whole house into darkness. A few minutes later the lights came back. The two women rushed to the dining table. The tablecloth had been changed. It bore the royal emblem of the Qutub Shahi Dynasty. The cutlery and crockery too had been changed. Instead of the simple Yera tumblers and the melamine plates, there were monogrammed, gold-edged plates and bowls and crystal glasses for water and wine. The dishes too had changed. There now was a delicious biryani. A mouth-watering salan. An oh-so-tempting array of kebabs. And bread ka meetha.

Shyamala Ma'am felt weak at her knees, and managed to sit down. Her friend too sat down next to her and started shivering. She had been told the story of the magic dishes appearing, you see. And while she didn't quite believe it when she was being told, she was now an eyewitness to the magic ... or the miracle.

Suddenly, the phone rang. The shrill ringing jerked them both out of the nervous calm that had descended on the house. 'Yes, who is it?' Shyamala Ma'am asked when she picked up the phone with great trepidation.

'Shyamala Ma'am, please open the door,' the caller asked. 'This is Qutub.'

'Qutub? Who Qutub?' Shyamala Ma'am asked.

'Quli Qutub Shah, the King ... of the Qutub Shahi Dynasty, the caller explained in a gravelly voice. Now open the door, Shyamala Devi,' it continued.

'Open the door! What nonsense, I don't open the door to strangers,' Shyamala Ma'am said bravely. 'And in any case you are speaking to me on the phone. I don't need to open the door to listen to you.'

'Open the door, you silly woman!' he roared. 'How dare you disobey me!'

Shyamala Ma'am knew when she was beaten. She gingerly walked to the door and opened it. She looked out carefully.

'Qutub!' she exclaimed when she saw young Qutub and Hyder waiting there. 'What are you doing here at this time of the night?'

It was Hyder who replied. 'We wanted to thank you, Shyamala Ma'am, for taking us to Charminar and Chowmohalla and all the other historic places. Also, we wanted to thank you for the way you helped Qutub when he had his fit.'

'No, no, that's perfectly okay. I was just ...' Shyamala Ma'am tried to make light of the whole episode.

'Nonsense,' said Qutub quite gently. And he placed a gift wrapped box into Shyamala Ma'am's hands ignoring her objections.

Then the two children said their salaams gracefully and turned around and left.

Shyamala Ma'am went back into her room and hesitantly opened the box they had given her. When she opened it, she got a shock.

The box was full of gold coins and exquisite jewellery. Also there was a thank you note written on a piece of paper that had the royal seal of the Qutub Shahi dynasty on it.

This is too much, she thought. And decided to confront the children the next day and insist on returning the costly gift to them.

When she walked into school the next day, she was surprised to see all the kids looking sad. Some were even crying. On enquiring what the matter was, she got a further shock.

Young Qutub and Hyder had died in a car accident the previous evening. They were on their way to Shyamala Ma'am's house with a box of sweets when a speeding bus had knocked them down and killed them.

While their bodies were smashed to pulp, the box of sweets escaped unhurt. But within minutes, the box had vanished. Some heartless soul had obviously stolen it from the scene of the accident. 'When ... when did this happen?' asked Shyamala Ma'am.

Thank you

'At about 4.30 p.m.,' replied the school principal who was there.

Shyamala Ma'am told herself in a slow, unbelieving kind of way ... but they came to my house at 8.30 p.m. And gave me, not a box of sweets but ...

Shyamala Ma'am never told any of her students a ghost story ... ever again.